Critical Thinking for Marketers

Critical Thinking for Marketers

Learn How to Think, Not What to Think

Volume II

David Dwight, Terry Grapentine, and
David Soorholtz

BEP BUSINESS EXPERT PRESS

Critical Thinking for Marketers: Learn How to Think, Not What to Think,
Volume II

Copyright © Business Expert Press, LLC, 2017.

First published in 2017 by
Business Expert Press, LLC
222 East 46th Street, New York, NY 10017
www.businessexpertpress.com

ISBN-13: 978-1-63157-670-6 (paperback)
ISBN-13: 978-1-63157-671-3 (e-book)

Business Expert Press Marketing Strategy Collection

Collection ISSN: 2150-9654 (print)
Collection ISSN: 2150-9662 (electronic)

Cover and interior design by Exeter Premedia Services Private Ltd., Chennai, India

First edition: 2017

10 9 8 7 6 5 4 3 2 1

Printed in the United States of America.

This book's vignettes are drawn, in part, from the authors' business experiences over a collective period of 105 years, during which time the authors flew a combined 6 million miles and spent over 10 years away from home. At times we left sick kids and other domestic responsibilities in the loving care of our life-long partners. Consequently, this book is dedicated to our wives:

Cindy Dwight, Jean Grapentine, and Shelly Soorholtz

Thank you for putting up with us and always welcoming us home.

Abstract

Volume I of *Critical Thinking for Marketers* focuses on helping you make strong and cogent marketing arguments. These arguments provide the foundation for strategic and tactical recommendations you ultimately will make to senior management or the board of directors.

In contrast, Volume II expands your background knowledge of other areas of critical thinking that are making major contributions to both marketing as a social science (what professors do) and marketing as an applied science (what you as real-world marketers do). This background knowledge should give you a better appreciation for how knowledge is created in marketing. Having a basic understanding of selected concepts in the fields of behavioral economics and cognitive science are vital to improving the quality of marketing decisions and recommendations you make on a daily basis.

This volume is divided into three major sections: Think Better, Cognitive Biases and Their Importance, and Conclusions.

Section I, Think Better, provides introductory discussions of

- Marketing as a science.
- The difference between correlation and causation, plus a thinking tool ("The Five Whys?") to help in discerning the difference.
- The meaning of what a "concept" is and why it is critical for marketers to develop good concept definitions (e.g., "What is *customer satisfaction?*").
- Why what the Scottish philosopher David Hume said 170 years ago is relevant to marketers today.
- The impact that behavioral economics is having on how marketers do their job.

Section II, Cognitive Biases and Their Importance, talks about recent discoveries in cognitive psychology and neuroscience that have relevance to marketers. You'll learn that marketers need to be aware of their own cognitive biases and irrational thinking processes, which often lead to making bad decisions, and that the retail and business customers we market to are not as rational as we may think and hope they are.

Finally, Section III, Conclusions, draws on both Volumes I and II to summarize the book's primary messages with helpful hints on applying your new tools and making better marketing decisions.

Keywords

behavioral economics, causation, cognitive biases, cognitive science, concept, correlation, critical thinking, epistemology, logic, marketing, marketing laws, science

Contents

Acknowledgments

Dr. Naresh K. Malhotra—Senior Fellow, Georgia Tech Center for International Business Education and Research; Regents' Professor Emeritus, Georgia Institute of Technology (Georgia Tech); and Editor, Review of Marketing Research—is responsible for encouraging us to research and ultimately write this book on critical thinking for marketers. His feedback and direction during the course of preparing the manuscript is greatly appreciated.

The following people provided valuable feedback and recommendations on previous drafts of this document: Kevin Gray, Cannon Gray LLC; Jean Grapentine; and, Terry Grapentine's long-time editor and friend, Lynn Coleman.

Kevin deLaplante, PhD, Founder and Lead Instructor, Critical Thinker Academy (http://kevindelaplante.com) graciously gave us permission to reprint selected sections from his Critical Thinker Academy website. Terry first met Kevin when he was an associate professor of philosophy at Iowa State University, Ames, where Terry and Kevin would occasionally discuss the philosophy of science, physics, critical thinking, and marketing, over drinks.

David Dwight
Terry Grapentine
David Soorholtz
July 2016

SECTION I
Think Better

CHAPTER 1

Introduction

The first Think Better piece, at the conclusion of Chapter 1 (Volume I), talks about the importance of background knowledge in developing one's critical thinking skills. Recall that *background knowledge* is the sum total of all our knowledge and experiences. In particular, increasing your background knowledge of marketing and logical fallacies will enhance your ability to develop good and persuasive marketing arguments. But that's just the beginning.

If you are committed to expanding your background knowledge you'll need to explore additional subject areas such as the philosophy of science, epistemology, marketing theory, behavioral economics, and heuristics. To this end, this chapter introduces you to selected topics in these fields:

- *Philosophy of Science*: This field studies what it means for a body of knowledge to be called a "science." The word *science* comes from the Latin, *Scientia*, meaning "to know." Most people associate the term *science* with the hard sciences— physics, chemistry, and biology—and are skeptical that a "soft" science such as sociology, economics, or marketing is deserving of that appellation. The Think Better piece, "Marketing as a Science," presents an argument claiming that, indeed, marketing is a science. Since a critical topic of all scientific inquiries is the nature of causation, the Think Better piece, "Correlation and Causation," provides an introduction to this subject.
- *Epistemology*: *The Stanford Encyclopedia of Philosophy* defines epistemology as "the study of knowledge and justified belief."[1] As such, epistemology is not completely separate from the philosophy of science. Often books on both topics cover similar material. The following Think Better pieces cover selected epistemological topics:

- ○ "What is a Concept" examines the nature of concepts and how they are defined.
- ○ "David Hume" introduces you to this 18th-century Scottish philosopher who wrote about how, if at all, inductive arguments can be justified.
- *Marketing Theory*: Byron Sharp and the researchers of the Ehrenberg-Bass Institute have written several books on marketing laws that their primary research, conducted over decades and supported by some of the world's largest marketing organizations, has uncovered. The Think Better piece, "The Double Jeopardy Law," introduces you to the nature of these laws, and the Double Jeopardy law in particular.
- *Behavioral Economics*: This Think Better piece of the same name provides an introduction to this field "of economic analysis that applies psychological insights into human behavior to explain economic decision-making."[2] A major finding of behavioral economists is that human beings' decision making is often "irrational," as that term is often construed, and this finding has significant implications for marketing.
- *Heuristics*: "A heuristic is any approach to problem solving, learning, or discovery that employs a practical method not guaranteed to be optimal or perfect, but sufficient for the immediate goals."[3] "The 5 Whys?" discusses this popular heuristic in solving marketing and business problems. Note that a list of 19 heuristic tools with discussions of their application to marketing is contained in Chapter 8 of Grapentine's book, *Applying Scientific Reasoning to the Field of Marketing*, which is referenced in the bibliography.

CHAPTER 2

Marketing as a Science

The word "science" can evoke an odd assortment of sensory fantasies in our minds—eccentric-looking individuals draped in white lab coats craning their necks over powerful microscopes or crouched over odd, diabolical-looking pieces of equipment, fiddling with dials and switches that emit strange crackling and buzzing sounds. A slight antiseptic smell wafts through the air. Chalk boards (yep, that shows our ages) marked with inscrutable mathematical equations hang silently from the walls. Yet we also realize that science gives birth to various applied disciplines of technology that infuse our lives with miraculous medicines, time-saving machines, and some really cool gadgets such as a new triathlon-watch with GPS, heart monitor, running pace, bike cadence, swimming stroke, and VO2-Max indicators.

The word "marketing" conjures different images: deadlines, sales quotas, advertising schedules, conferences, conventions, and meetings ... seemingly unending meetings—certainly nothing as romantic as receiving the Nobel Prize or patenting a lifesaving drug.

Yet, marketing is also a science as well as an applied discipline. Knowing why will actually help you improve the quality of your judgments and make more rational decisions than you would otherwise.[1] Let's explore why this is the case.

Clearly, marketing is an applied discipline. It is "applied" because marketers use the principles of marketing—often introduced in one's first college marketing class—to fashion and shape the "marketing mix." Oldies but goodies like the 4 Ps, that's what marketers do. Marketing is also a "discipline" because it contains an organized body of knowledge and an ongoing research program at universities around the world. It's what marketing professors do.

But does having an organized body of knowledge and ongoing research make marketing a "science?" After all, one could argue that astrology possesses an organized body of knowledge and ongoing research program, but few people would agree that astrology is a "science."

Defining what is and what is not a "science" is actually quite difficult, and we will not delve into the finer points of that subject in this book. Nonetheless, we offer a preliminary argument that marketing is a science and that knowing something about this science will make you a better marketer and critical thinker.

What aspects of marketing as a science are important for applied marketers to know? Well, there are many, and one of this book's authors, Terry Grapentine, wrote a treatise on this subject that is part of Business Expert Press' Marketing Strategy Collection: *Applying Scientific Reasoning to the Field of Marketing: Make Better Decisions*. Short of giving you a book review, this Think Better piece briefly discusses the following three aspects of marketing as a science that are important for you to know: (1) marketing concepts, models, and metrics; (2) marketing laws; and (3) the scientific way of thinking.

Marketing Concepts, Models, and Metrics

Since another Think Better piece, "What is a Concept?" addressed that topic, let's address the other two aspects of marketing as a science here: models and metrics.

Marketing models are conceptual or mathematical frameworks that attempt to identify factors called *independent* variables, which predict a useful marketing outcome variable, such as market share or product sales, also known as a *dependent* variable. A *marketing metric* "is a measuring system that quantifies a trend, dynamic, or [market-related] characteristic."[2]

Having some familiarity with marketing concepts, models, and metrics is important because they form the premises of marketing arguments. You don't need to be able to describe them at parties—just keep a good college-level marketing and advertising textbook on your shelf for reference.

Marketing Models

Advertising works in different ways and there are different *marketing models* that specifically describe this process, including the Awareness, Interest,

Desire, and Action (AIDA) model, the hierarchy of effects model, the information adoption model, and others.[3]

For example, the *standard learning model* is best suited for products where consumers display "high involvement," such as when they purchase automobiles or other relatively expensive durable goods (products that last a year or more). This model views the customer as an active participant in learning about new products. "Ads for products and services in these areas are usually very detailed and provide customers with information that can be used to evaluate brands and help them make a purchase decision."[4]

In contrast, we know of a property casualty insurance company whose advertising efforts are informed by the *dissonance/attribution model*. One aspect of that model suggests that an important role of advertising is to make customers comfortable about their purchase after the sale (i.e., reduce dissonance) so that they are more likely to renew their policy when it comes up for renewal.

Other kinds of models you may benefit from having a basic familiarity with include:

- *Marketing mix models* that help optimize your allocation of expenditures across different communications media such as television advertising, direct mail, and digital.
- *Price elasticity models* that help to determine the most profitable price for a product.
- *Innovation and diffusion models* that help you identify the early adopters of a new, innovative product.

In all cases, these models and their outputs create, in part, the premises of marketing arguments. And good premises go a long way to convince your audience of your recommendations.

Marketing Metrics

Marketing managers are interested in measuring their organization's marketing performance over time (the dependent variables discussed earlier) and all factors affecting that performance (independent variables). There are many kinds of metrics to do this. Examples include market penetration, unaided awareness, loyalty, sales force effectiveness, and incremental sales/promotion lift. Paul W. Farris et al. wrote a popular book on this topic called *Marketing Metrics: 50 + Metrics Every Executive Should Master.*[5]

Why will you benefit from being familiar with these metrics? Because, as Farris et al. say:

> Often, managers must decide whether to seek sales growth by acquiring existing category users from their competitors or by expanding the total population of category users, [by] attracting new customers to the market. Penetration metrics help indicate which of these strategies would be most appropriate and help managers to monitor their success.[6]

These metrics and their outputs create, in part, the premises of marketing arguments. And good premises help to convince your audience of your recommendations.

Marketing Laws

You may be familiar with some "laws" from the field of physics such as "no object can go faster than the speed of light." A *law* is a kind of necessity in nature. Regarding the speed of light, it's not that objects don't travel faster than the speed of light; it's that they *can't*—it's the law!

Marketing has "laws," too; if it did not, markets would be totally chaotic and unpredictable. Marketing laws are perhaps better characterized as *empirical regularities* that are probabilistic, not deterministic, in nature.

For example, consider the "user bases seldom vary" law. This law states that "rival brands sell to very similar customer bases."[7] So, the consumer demographics of those who purchase Energizer brand batteries look pretty much the same as consumers who purchase Duracell batteries. But this relationship is not deterministic. *Deterministic* means that if 20 percent of consumers who purchase the Energizer brand have yearly household incomes of $30,000 or less, then *exactly* 20 percent of the consumers who purchase the Duracell brand will be in the same income bracket. It is only possible that this will be case and that the actual percentages for both brands will be in the neighborhood of 20 percent, but very unlikely that it will be exactly so.

Why is this law important to know? Because many marketers tend to believe that their situation is unique—that their customers are different from competitors' customers and that a company needs to develop advertising messages uniquely designed for "our customers." Research shows that those strategies affect sales far less than would investing time and resources into efforts targeted to all potential customers in a market and increasing the "mental availability" (i.e., salience) of your brand. Byron Sharp discusses this at length in his award-winning book, *How Brands Grow: What Marketers Don't Know*.[8] In it, Sharp discusses the nature of 11 different marketing laws and how they affect a brand's market performance. One of these laws is the "user bases seldom vary law." Our Think Better piece on the Double Jeopardy law is also one of the 11 marketing laws that Sharp discusses in his book.

The Scientific Way of Thinking

We don't want to confuse the "the scientific method" with "the scientific way of thinking." The *scientific method* (TSM) is typically defined as follows:

> Scientific researchers propose hypotheses as explanations of phenomena and design experimental studies to test these hypotheses via predictions which can be derived from them. These steps must be repeatable, to guard against mistakes or confusion in any particular experiment.[9]

A good example of TSM is drug studies conducted for FDA approval in which the drug is compared to a placebo or for the treatment of a particular disease.

The *scientific way of thinking* (TSWT) is much broader than TSM. It's not a process or procedure, but rather an overarching way of looking at things. Scientific thinking in our field involves such activities as building one's background knowledge of marketing and the other fields that contribute to marketing knowledge (e.g., behavioral economics), applying good deductive and inductive logic to problem solving, avoiding logical fallacies, developing useful marketing concepts and strong arguments, and building theories that explain and predict marketing phenomenon.[10]

> If marketing is to plow the conceptual field that has so amazingly nurtured scientific discovery, we need to learn how to apply scientific reasoning to solving business problems. This means becoming familiar with some of the critical thinking tools that drive scientific discovery. This goal is not academic. Rather, it is one of the most practical endeavors a marketer can pursue, and might help us avoid making the same kind of mistake [we often read about in publications such as *Forbes* and *The Wall Street Journal*].[11]

Bottom line: The purpose of this book is to help you develop strong and cogent marketing arguments. A critical aspect of this task is to incorporate into your arguments' premises, relevant marketing concepts, models, and metrics that will give your audience good reasons to believe your recommendations.

But you will be hampered in these efforts unless you strive to build your understanding and knowledge in these subject areas and their unique vocabularies. This is one of the dirty little secrets of critical thinking: *Learning how to construct truth-conducive arguments that also persuade your audience to accept your recommendations takes time and effort. No silver bullets here.*

CHAPTER 3

Correlation and Causation

Perhaps no single concept is more pervasive and important in marketing than the notion of cause and effect. Marketing practitioners depend on it in the planning and implementation of programs designed to obtain responses from consumers. Ideas of advertising affecting sales, opinion leaders influencing the adoption of new products, or promotion activities producing interest and preferences for one's wares all rely implicitly on mechanisms of cause and effect.[1]

Many of the logical fallacies in this book, such as Alleged Certainty, the Hasty Generalization, and Affirming the Consequent, are influenced by the cardinal sin of equating correlation with causation. How do you tell the difference between mere correlation and true causation?

Let's first define "causation": when one event will or can bring about another. One of the most common cause and effect relationships in marketing is reflected in the law of supply and demand—price reductions generally cause more consumers to purchase a product. There are three necessary criteria for saying that one variable is a cause of another: (1) temporal sequence, (2) concomitant variation, and (3) absence of other possible causes. All three conditions must be met to substantiate a causative relationship.

Temporal Sequence

If P causes Q, then P must occur before or at the same time as Q. Sometimes it's difficult to say which comes first, as described by Malhotra:

> For example, customers who shop frequently in a department store are more likely to have the credit card for that store. Also, customers who have a department store's credit card are likely to

shop there frequently. The time order of these variables—credit card ownership and frequent shopping—is not obvious. Did shopping precede credit card ownership? An understanding of the underlying phenomena associated with department store shopping might be necessary to accurately identify time order.[2]

Concomitant Variation

If P is a cause of Q, then the values of P and Q are correlated in the same direction. If the value of P increases, the value of Q increases, and vice versa. For example, if you expect that sales force quality is a cause of sales, then as the quality of the sales force increases (decreases), sales will increase (decrease) too, all other factors held constant.

Absence of Other Causal Factors

In a simple example of this condition, if P is hypothesized to cause Q, there are no other true causes of Q that happen to be correlated with both P and Q. Consider Figure 3.1 below.

In this example, an increase in social media spending (P) is hypothesized to cause an increase in sales (Q), which is denoted by the solid arrow from P to Q—solid arrows denote a possible causative relationship.

During this time period, however, the company also deployed a sales training program (R). There is dashed arrow from R to P denoting that these two variables are merely correlated and that changes in R do not *cause* changes in P.

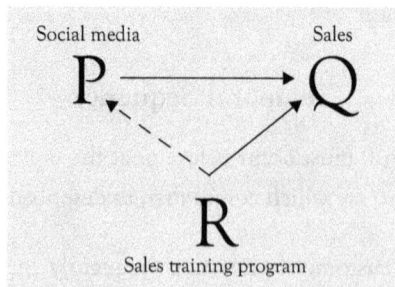

Figure 3.1 *Causal pathways*

In contrast, there is solid arrow pointing from R to Q denoting that an increase in the quality of the sales force via a training program (R) could cause an increase in sales (Q).

But from the information provided, it's impossible to infer what causes Q to increase. Do only changes in P cause changes in Q, only changes in R cause changes in Q, or do changes in both P and R cause changes in Q?

Most situations in marketing are similar to the above example—multiple events occur in markets at approximately the same time, which makes inferring causation problematic.

This does not, however, give one license to start using logical fallacies with abandon! For example, someone might employ the Affirming the Consequent fallacy to make the case that an increase in social media spending causes sales to increase by saying: "If our social media campaign were effective, then sales should increase. Sales increased. Therefore our social media campaign was effective." This is poor reasoning because factors other than the social media campaign could have caused sales to increase.

Correlation, Causation, and Logical Fallacies

Short of running experimental research in which you hold constant or otherwise take into account all other factors except the one you are testing to determine causality, how do you avoid making erroneous causal claims? There is no simple answer to this question. In the above example, marketing research may reveal—for example, by interviewing customers—whether the sales training program or the social media campaign more likely explains an increase or decrease in sales. If you can't conduct a marketing research study, you will need to construct alternative hypotheses—there is always more than one explanation for a set of data—and select the one that best explains the market behavior you've observed. This is called Inference to the Best Explanation (IBE). Among the competing hypotheses, select the strongest and most cogent one.

Interaction Effects and INUS Conditions

Identifying or inferring causation can become more problematic if interaction effects occur. An *interaction effect* is a condition in which a factor's influence on a marketing outcome is affected by the presence of another factor. In the aforesaid example, maybe sales would increase only if a change were made *both* in social media *and* sales force training—no one action by itself would be decisive. There would be an interaction effect between social media and sales training when both have to be present to affect sales.

It gets worse! As described by Terry Grapentine in his book, *Applying Scientific Reasoning to the Field of Marketing: Make Better Decisions*, a single factor or group of factors—called a *condition*—may be either necessary or insufficient to influence a consumer to consider a brand. There are always some *necessary* conditions that have to be met for a consumer to consider a product. Clearly, if consumers cannot find a product, they cannot buy it. Product availability (X) is a necessary condition for purchase (Y). X, however, may be a necessary condition, but it may be *insufficient* by itself to bring about a purchase. The product also must be competitively priced—making X both a necessary and "insufficient condition" to motivate purchase.

Most causes of consumer purchasing behavior can be attributed to INUS conditions—**I**nsufficient **N**ecessary **U**nnecessary **S**ufficient, as explained by Richard Bagozzi (italics added):

> As an example, let us examine the claim sometimes made by marketers that brand image (measured by the brand name) affects the perception of quality. When marketers make this claim they are not saying that the brand image is a necessary cause or condition for the attribution of quality. One may judge a product as high or low in quality without knowing the brand. Similarly, marketers are not claiming that the brand image is sufficient for the perception of quality since one must at least attend to, be aware of, and evaluate the brand name before such an attribution can be made. Rather, the brand image may be regarded as an INUS condition in that it is an insufficient but necessary part of a condition that is itself unnecessary but sufficient for the result. Many of the causal relations investigated by marketers are of this sort.[3]

The lesson to be learned with respect to not confusing correlation with causation when developing marketing strategies and tactics is this: Be mindful of the complexities of causality when making marketing arguments. Use evidence to support your causal claims.

CHAPTER 4

What Is a Concept?

"How *satisfied* are customers with our service?" "We want to exceed our customers' *expectations*." "We need to discover what is *important* to our customers." "Are our customers more *loyal* than our competitors' customers?" "We need to improve our *product quality*."

How can we as marketers answer these questions if the *concepts* in the questions—satisfaction, expectations, importance—are vague or ambiguous? Your first thought is likely to associate the term *concept* with the words "things" or "ideas." For example, "loyalty" and "satisfaction" are ideas. A "customer" and "products" are "things." But this begs the following questions: "What is an idea? What is a thing?"

In a broader sense, "concepts" encompass "things" and "ideas," and are major *building blocks* of communication along with other parts of speech that we learned in grammar school such as verbs, adjectives, and prepositions. It is this broader definition that we apply in the context of this book. But, "what really *is* a concept?" Let's take a look.

First, you need to appreciate the fact that the word "concept" has deep roots in the philosophy of science and linguistics. It is a highly complex topic. Consequently, the objective of this Think Better piece is to help you gain an appreciation for the *complexity* of concepts in general and marketing concepts in particular, so that when you use them in future marketing communications, you'll do a good job of defining them.

A *concept* categorizes a certain aspect of reality. For example, the term *chair* is a concept. The aspects of reality it includes are certain objects we sit on. We include in the category "chair" such objects as an Adirondack chair, an armchair, a Captain's chair, a folding chair, and so on. A "concept" is defined by its properties. Some properties of a chair include: one or more legs or leg-type structures supporting a seating area, a back support; a seating area parallel to the ground on which one bends slightly to sit down. If an object possesses these properties, we call it a chair. It is much easier to ask someone for a chair than it is to ask someone for an object that combines each of its properties. And of course, each property is itself a concept. Consequently, it is impossible to communicate without concepts.

So let's take a common concept we deal with as marketers: "satisfaction." Often, marketers will define "satisfaction" to mean "when a customer is satisfied." But this is not a good definition because the term *satisfaction* is used to define the concept "satisfaction." It's kind of like saying "hot" means "hot." Also, this definition does not help us understand what the properties of "satisfaction" are, the way that the definition of "chair" tells us what the properties of a chair are. And before you try to second guess what the definition of "satisfaction" is, we'll tell you right now that the definition is complicated and not everyone in marketing agrees about what it is![1] Don't feel bad. There are undoubtedly those who would argue over our definition of "chair" also. However, this does not mean that we suggest throwing our hands up in despair because it's impossible to agree on the definitions of a given term. It does mean that, in defining concepts, the parties involved must take the time to develop good definitions before seeking to take action on the concept (e.g., to improve customer "satisfaction").

Originally, marketer's definitions of "satisfaction" focused on the issue of customer expectations, where *expectation* is defined as a forecast of performance. For example, if you expect to wait in line for two minutes at a bank teller's drive-up window, and you only wait one minute, your expectation is *disconfirmed* positively—your wait is less than your forecast—and, as a result, you experience positive satisfaction. Conversely, if you wait three minutes, your expectation is *disconfirmed* negatively, and you experience negative satisfaction. In a sense, it is this disconfirmation and whether it is positive or negative that is "satisfaction." In other words, one way to define "satisfaction" without using the term *satisfaction* is to say that *satisfaction* is the difference between (i.e., the disconfirmation of) forecasted and actual product performance at a particular point in time. Note: this definition can be extended to include the product or service as a whole, or certain aspects of a product of service.

Alternative definitions of satisfaction might focus on (a) this concept's emotional component, such as whether a customer "likes" a product, or (b) the extent to which a product meets a customer's needs and wants.

The Giese and Cote article cited in the endnote of this discussion identifies 20 different definitions of satisfaction found in the recent marketing literature.

The point we're making is that "satisfaction" is a complicated concept, there are different ways of defining it, and the different ways of defining it affect how an organization measures satisfaction and ultimately answers the question, *"How do we improve customer satisfaction?"* If the brand manager is using definition #3—a customer "likes" a product—and the sales manager is using definition #14—a product exceeds a customer's "expectation"—you can see where problems can arise! For example, a customer may "like" a product, but the product does not exceed the customer's forecast of product performance.

The question of *"What definition of satisfaction should management focus on?"* is even more complicated than suggested in the foregoing discussion. Some researchers have pointed out that satisfied customers do not always purchase the same brand over time; and that a more useful concept for management is "loyalty," not "satisfaction."[2] But this begs the question, *"How do you define loyalty?"* Some researchers define it as the percentage of times a consumer purchases a target brand over a given time period. Others define it as the likelihood a consumer will purchase a target brand in the future. Just as for the "satisfaction" concept, there are many definitions of "loyalty."

So let's return to our definition of a concept. It is easy to see that an object like a chair has physical properties that can be observed—legs, a sitting surface, and a back support. Although it is possible to debate which of those properties should be used in describing the concept of a chair, we can at least *see* what we are debating. But what are the properties of mental states such as "satisfaction"? As an example, let's go back to our earlier definition: the difference between forecasted and actual product performance at a given point in time. The properties of this definition of satisfaction are as follows:

- *Time*: Satisfaction occurs at a particular point in time when a product is used or consumed; say at time "t."
- *Forecasted performance*: A forecast of the perceived performance of a product at time "t."

- *Actual performance*: The perceived product performance at time "t."
- *Difference*: The subtraction of the perceived performance measure from the forecasted performance measure.

These properties of "satisfaction," therefore, are used to define that term.

The process of defining the properties of marketing concepts is both complex and difficult, but we don't mean to imply that to be a good critical marketing thinker you need to have a PhD in marketing and be familiar with the marketing literature on concept development. *But you do need to appreciate that these concepts are multifaceted and when you use them in drafting, say, a marketing strategy, you need to have some sense of this complexity and some basis for choosing the particular definition of a concept that you're using.*

You and your team will benefit from agreeing on the definitions of concepts such as "satisfaction" or "importance" before using them to measure your business' performance. A good starting point for further learning is to get your hands on a good marketing text book. We recommend Byron Sharp's (2013) *Marketing: Theory, Evidence, Practice,* Oxford University Press. If you want to pursue this topic in greater detail, we additionally recommend reading the following:

- Grapentine, Terry (2015), "Get what I mean? How to think about constructs in marketing research," *Quirks Marketing Research Review,* August, pp. 40–46.
- Kerlinger, Fred N., and Howard B. Lee (2000), *Foundations of Behavioral Research, 4th Edition,* Harcourt College Publishers, New York, especially Chapter 3: Constructs, Variables, and Definitions, pp. 41–62.
- Zaltman, Gerald, Chrstian R. A. Pinson, and Reinhard Angelmar (1973), *Metatheory and Consumer Research,* Holt, Rinehart and Winston, New York, p. 22.
- Bottom line: poorly defined concepts = muddled thinking.

CHAPTER 5

David Hume

Any proper discussion of causation needs to invoke the 18th-century Scottish philosopher, David Hume (1711 to 1776), and what has come to be called "Hume's problem of induction." Ideas expressed in *An Inquiry Concerning Human Understanding* (1748) over 250 years ago have relevance for today's marketers. Let's first examine the problem of induction from a general perspective, and then investigate its application to marketing.

Generally, the problem of induction states that there is no justification to believe that the patterns historically observed will continue into the future. This may seem to be a ridiculous proposition since we all believe that the sun will rise tomorrow, balls drop to the ground, and hot air rises. However, Hume contends that what we observe in nature is one thing following another—what is sometimes called *constant conjunction*. We attribute causation to patterns we observe because of our psychological disposition to do so—it helps us to make order of things.

The key to understanding Hume's point-of-view is to appreciate the use of the term, *justification*, and to accept the fact that, in many situations, Hume is indeed correct. Often, we are not *justified* in assuming one event will follow another. For example, I am not an automotive engineer and, consequently, I have no *good justification* to believe that my car will start the next time I turn the ignition key, simply because it has always done so in the past. This is circular logic because the premise of my argument, "my car always starts," assumes the truth of my conclusion, "therefore, my car will start in the future." I may indeed be correct, but I have not given a *good reason* to support my conclusion.

Many businesses stick to the same old business models (i.e., "arguments"), believing that what worked yesterday will work tomorrow—Kodak, AOL, General Motors, Borders Books, Merrill Lynch,

Montgomery Ward, and the list goes on. In marketing, however, generally what has worked in the past does not work indefinitely into the future.

What, then, can critical thinkers learn from David Hume? Do not assume that historical patterns will repeat themselves unless you have good evidence supporting that claim. In short, avoid the following kind of logic in an argument:

> *X happened historically*
> Therefore, X will happen tomorrow.

If you think that X will happen tomorrow, find some basis for this claim. For example, if X is your company's recent historical growth rate, perhaps X is theoretically related to your country's population growth rate. Linking X to an authority's predicted population growth rate then gives you some grounds for saying that some level of X is likely to happen in the future.

Remember: Just because something happens with some historical frequency is not sufficient justification to say that it will continue to do so in the future.

CHAPTER 6

The Double Jeopardy Law

Knowledge of marketing theories, such as the Double Jeopardy Law (and others discussed throughout this book) are useful in creating premises for arguments supporting marketing strategies.

In the Appeal to Possibility discussion, Jacqueline and Conner ponder how to increase their shampoo brand's market share. They know that market share, over a given period of time, is a function of the number of customers who purchase a brand (i.e., market penetration) and the frequency of brand purchase. They want to increase their brand's share and, to achieve that goal, believe it will be easier to increase the brand's purchase frequency than the number of consumers who will purchase it. Their Appeal to Possibility, Appeal to Ignorance, and a misunderstanding of how market penetration and purchase frequency are related have led them to a bad conclusion.

If they had been aware of the Double Jeopardy Law, Jacqueline and Conner could have made a better argument supporting a different brand growth strategy. The Double Jeopardy Law states that

> smaller market share brands are penalized twice; not only have they fewer customers who buy them (their penetration is smaller than that of big brands), but also customers who do buy them do so less often—and, in memory metrics, less popular brands are known by fewer people and those people are slightly less likely to say that they like it.[1]

Based on analysis from the Ehrenberg-Bass Institute,[2] in many situations, the key to increasing market share is to increase penetration, not to increase purchase frequency among those currently purchasing the product. Had Jacqueline and Conner been aware of this law, they could have reframed their suggested strategy to increase market share by

Table 6.1 Market share, market penetration, and purchase frequency across selected shampoo brands[3]

Shampoo brands	Market share (%)	Annual market penetration (%)	Purchase frequency (average)
Head & Shoulders	11	13	2.3
Pantene	9	11	2.3
Herbal Essences	5	8	1.8
L'Oreal Elvive	5	8	1.9
Dove	5	9	1.6
Sunsilk	5	8	1.7
Vosene	2	3	1.7

focusing on increasing the brand's penetration, not the brand's purchase frequency among current customers.

Researchers have observed the Double Jeopardy Law across a variety of industries such as consumer packaged goods (e.g., what you find in the grocery store), durable goods (e.g., vehicles and electronics products), and services. Table 6.1 shows how market share, annual market penetration, and purchase frequency compare for selected shampoo brands.

Note that all three columns of figures are highly correlated. The theory and empirical evidence suggest that market penetration drives market share and purchase frequency. But if one is not aware of the Double Jeopardy Law, one might attempt to develop a marketing strategy that seeks to increase market share by increasing purchase frequency, which is highly unlikely to be effective.

Byron Sharp discusses 11 marketing laws in his book *How Brands Grow*. You should be familiar with them, as well as with the *Journal of Empirical Generalizations in Marketing Science* at //empgens.com/ArticlesHome/Articles.html

Remember: Some marketing strategies not only don't work. They can't work. It's the law!

CHAPTER 7

Behavioral Economics

Many recent bestselling books have forced marketers and marketing researchers to rethink the motivations they attribute to consumers—books such as *Freakonomics*, by Steven D. Levitt and Stephen J. Dubner; *Predictably Irrational: The Hidden Forces That Shape Our Decisions*, by Dan Ariely; and Malcom Gladwell's *The Tipping Point: How Little Things Can Make a Big Difference*. We no longer think of either retail consumers, like you and me, or business decision-makers as *homo economicus* (economic man)—that phantom of classical economics, the unemotional, value-maximizing buyer of goods and services, whose computer brain, with perfect market information, activates sophisticated product attribute/price trade-off algorithms prior to every purchase.

In forming strong and cogent marketing arguments whose premises reference consumer motivations, you need to know something about Behavioral Economics. For example, consider a project that one of the authors conducted for a global cell phone manufacturer some years ago. Standard marketing research methods such as focus groups, one-on-one interviews, and quantitative surveys painted cell phone purchasers as the classic *homo economicus* consumer. Cell phone owners reported being "rational" decision-makers, carefully evaluating not only the various product features of cell phones, but also the various carrier service plans. Plugging all this information into their CPU brains, consumers indicated they chose the phone and plan that "maximized their utility."

However, an ethnographic study in which consumers were observed evaluating and purchasing their phones (and later interviewed while their phone was being programmed) revealed the image of *homo economicus* to be an apparition. In reality, a significant segment of cell phone buyers were confused by all the product choices and carrier plans available. In place of cranking up their computer algorithms, after a short conversation with the store's sales rep, they simply purchased the phone and plan recommended by the rep. In short, they were acting more like a dumb robot than an Artifical Intelligence android. Study findings significantly affected how this company marketed to the end consumer. For instance, they redoubled their efforts in educating store clerks on the company's new phones and worked with their channel members to display their phones in a way that facilitated consumer education as opposed to striking confusion in their minds.

In short, what behavioral economics is teaching marketers is that the context in which a purchase is made—the surrounding environment, consumer emotions, and situational factors—can have as much influence on purchase choice as do a product's price and features. Yes, several studies have shown that playing French music in a liquor store spikes the sale of French wines.[1] And if product offers are perceived to be too confusing, consumers will often not make a purchase. A study conducted by a friend of one of the authors for a national luggage manufacturer discovered that their placards placed in front of product displays in department stores were being ignored, thus causing lost sales. De-briefing consumers after they purchased a competing product uncovered that the company's placards simply contained too much information. Many consumers were gravitating toward brands with simple or no signage at all.

The central point of these Think Better pieces is to emphasize the importance of *background knowledge* in strengthening your ability as a marketer to make sound and cogent arguments. Simply sharpening your logic skills so that you can quickly catch a colleague using a logical fallacy is not enough to be a good critical thinker. More than ever before, marketing knowledge is being informed by fields such as behavioral economics, neuroscience, psychology, and anthropology. We can't be experts in all these areas, but we can at least acquaint ourselves with them by reading in our field, attending marketing conferences, and talking with our colleagues about what they've learned and how they think it applies to their situations.

Make more rational marketing arguments by understanding the often irrational consumer to whom you are marketing.

CHAPTER 8

The Five Whys

Developed in the 1930s by Sakichi Toyoda as part of The Toyota Production System, the Five Whys help identify root causes of problems.

In the context of this book, the method helps managers discover factors contributing to a marketing problem around which solutions can be formulated. Recall that a solution to a marketing problem takes the form of an argument—given *premises* X, Y, and Z (in part derived from asking the Five Whys), we therefore should do A, the argument's *conclusion*.

Here's a hypothetical example: Let's assume that customers are complaining about poor product quality. We pose a series of Five Whys and answers such as the following:

1. Why? *We are not effectively catching manufacturing errors before products are shipped.*
2. Why? *Ineffective communication between quality control and manufacturing.*
3. Why? Often, *quality control reports are getting to manufacturing too late.*
4. Why? *Quality control reports are written on paper and sent via intra-company mail. Sometimes, manufacturing doesn't get these reports until product is shipped to the warehouse, and then off to the customer.*
5. Why? *There is no procedure in place to ensure that product lots are not released to the warehouse until the quality control documents have been reviewed by manufacturing's shipping department.*

Presumably these five answers can serve as premises to an argument whose conclusion is: "Therefore, the shipping department manager must review quality control reports and not release products for shipment to the warehouse unless the quality control report estimates that less than 1 percent of the products in a lot are defective."

Six Sigma programs have integrated the Five Whys into:

... the Analyze phase of the Six Sigma DMAIC (Define, Measure, Analyze, Improve, Control) methodology. It is a great ... tool that does not involve data segmentation, hypothesis testing, regression or other advanced statistical tools, and in many cases can be completed without a data collection plan.[1]

But the Five Whys is not without its critics. Some complaints[2] about this tool are:

- It may take more than Five Whys to get at the root problem, and there is a bias to stop at five because of the technique's name.
- The tool often needs input from different departments or functions in an organization. Different departments may answer the Five Whys differently.
- There is a tendency to identify only one root cause of a problem. Often, complicated problems have multiple root causes.

These are relevant criticisms; however, there is no single method that can identify all the causal factors and relationships associated with complex problems. The Five Whys may need to be supplemented with other tools, such as conducting specific research projects that examine one or more processes within an organization. Nevertheless, the Five Whys can be one of many tools marketing managers use to get to the root cause of marketing problems.

SECTION II

Cognitive Biases and Their Importance

CHAPTER 9

Introduction

Cognitive bias is a "systematic error in judgment and decision making common to all human beings, which can be due to cognitive limitations, motivational factors, and/or adaptations to natural environments."[1] Some of the logical fallacies discussed earlier in this book can be a source of cognitive bias, such as interpreting correlation as causation in the Affirming the Consequent fallacy. Other sources are covered in some of the Think Better sections (see the discussion on Behavioral Economics). But could another source be the very evolutionary processes that created us *homo sapiens*?

Having a comprehensive understanding of all these sources of cognitive biases helps us develop "epistemic humility," which is being humble about the knowledge we *think* we possess, and which is a necessary requirement for being a good critical thinker.

The remainder of this section is excerpted from Kevin deLaplante's discussion of cognitive biases, which can be found on his Critical Thinking Academy website.[2] We include it in our book because it is an excellent and relevant discussion of this subject matter.

Additionally, at various points in this section, we include shaded sidebar discussions focusing on how deLaplante's article relates to critical thinking in marketing.

* * *

CHAPTER 10

What They Are and Why They're Important

Everyone agrees that logic and argumentation are important for critical thinking. (And an important component of improving one's critical thinking skills is) *background knowledge* ....

There are different types of background knowledge that are relevant to critical thinking in different ways. One of the most important types of background knowledge is knowledge of how our minds actually work—how human beings actually think and reason, how we actually form beliefs, how we actually make decisions.

There are a lot of different scientific fields that study how our minds actually work. These include *behavioral psychology*, *social psychology*, *cognitive psychology*, *cognitive neuroscience*, and other fields. Over the past 40 years we've learned an awful lot about human reasoning and decision making.

A lot of this research was stimulated by the work of two important researchers, Daniel Kahneman and Amos Tversky, going back to the early 1970s. They laid the foundations for what is now called the "biases and heuristics" tradition in psychology.[1]

Normative Versus Descriptive Theories of Human Reasoning

To get a feel for the importance of this research, let's back up a bit. When studying human reasoning you can ask two sorts of question. One is a purely *description* question—how *do* human beings *in fact* reason? The other is a *prescriptive* or *normative* question—how *should* human beings reason? What's the difference between *good* reasoning and *bad* reasoning?

When we study logic and argumentation, we're learning a set of rules and concepts that permit us to answer this *second* question—how *should* we reason ....

... [O]ver time, we've developed a number of different theories of rationality that give us norms for correct reasoning in different domains.

This is great, of course, (as) these are very powerful and useful tools. (Some of which are the focus of this book).

Now, when it comes to the study of how human reasoning *actually* works, before Kahneman and Tversky's work in the 1970s, there was a widely shared view that, more often than not, the mind, or the brain, processes information in ways that mimic the formal models of reasoning and decision making that were familiar from our normative models of reasoning, from formal logic, probability theory, and decision theory.

> *This "widely shared view" has influenced the methods marketing research-ers often use. For example, three commonly used methods researchers employ to model brand choice are (1) conjoint analysis, (2) regression analysis, or (3) the combination of brand attribute performance ratings with attribute "importance" ratings. Findings from behavioral economics suggest that these kinds of models do not tell us the complete story—in fact they may weave a false story—of how consumers select brands. In short, consumers are not as "rational" as we think they are.*

What Kahneman and Tversky showed is that, more often than not, this is NOT the way our minds work—they showed that there's a gap between how our normative theories say we *should* reason and how we *in fact* reason.

This gap can manifest itself in different ways, and there's no one single explanation for it. One reason, for example, is that in real-world situa-tions, the reasoning processes prescribed by our normative theories of rationality can be computationally very intensive. Our brains would need to process an awful lot of information to implement our best normative theories of reasoning. But that kind of information processing takes time, and in the real world we often need to make decisions much quicker, sometimes in milliseconds. You can imagine this time pressure being even more intense if you think about the situations facing our *homo sapiens* ancestors; if there's a big animal charging you and you wait too long to figure out what to do, you're dead.

> *This is an important point for marketers. Often, marketing managers need to make relatively quick decisions based on either too little or too much information. This frequently leads to using "rules of thumb" that we fall back on to save time. These shortcuts in making decisions are called "heuristics"—practical, time-saving processes used to make quick decisions that are not necessary optimal or perfect. Sometimes, these heuristics employ one or more of the 60 logical fallacies discussed in this book—and when they do, you can be certain that the likelihood of a bad decision being made will increase. Note that a "heuristic" can also refer to ways "for thinking about phenomena or questions in a way that might give you new insights and ideas,"[2] which can be used in argument development. Our Think Better piece on The Five Whys is an example.*

Biases and Heuristics (Rules of Thumb)

So, the speculation is that our brains have evolved various *short-cut mechanisms for making decisions*, especially when the problems we're facing are complex, we have incomplete information, and there's risk involved. In these situations we sample the information available to us, we focus on just those bits that are most relevant to our decision task, and we make a decision based on a rule of thumb, or a shortcut, that does the job.

These rules of thumb are the "heuristics" in the "biases and heuristics" literature.

Two important things to note: One is that we're usually not consciously aware of the heuristics that we're using, or the information that we're focusing on. *Most of this is going on below the surface.*

The second thing to note is these heuristics *aren't* designed to give us the *best* solutions to our decision problems, all things considered. What they're designed to do is give us solutions that are "good enough" for our immediate purposes.

But "good enough" might mean "good enough in our ancestral environments where these cognitive mechanisms evolved." In contexts that are more removed from those ancestral environments (say in a marketing committee), we can end up making systematically bad choices or errors in reasoning, because we're automatically, subconsciously invoking the heuristic in a situation where that heuristic isn't necessarily the best rule to follow.

So, the term *bias* in this context refers to this systematic *gap* between how we're *actually disposed* to behave or reason, and how we *ought* to behave or reason, by the standards of some normative theory of reasoning or decision-making. The "heuristic" is the *rule of thumb* that we're using to make the decision or the judgment; the "bias" is the *predictable effect* of *using* that rule of thumb in situations where it doesn't give an optimal result.

Some examples of heuristics in marketing decision-making we've observed are as follows:

- *"What's happened in the past will happen tomorrow": For example, making financial projections based simply on historical trends and not taking into account other factors that can affect future financial performance, such as projected GNP growth or the prime interest rate.*
- *Argument to moderation: "Splitting the difference" between alternative marketing projections (e.g., a sales forecast) because one does not have sufficient time to develop a better forecast supported by good evidence and logic.*
- *"Shooting from the hip": Simply guessing what action to take because one does not have enough time to properly investigate a particular issue.*
- *Alleged certainty: Relying on conventional wisdom—"Everyone knows that …"—to make a decision as opposed to thinking through a problem in greater detail.*

An Example: The Anchoring Effect

This is all pretty general, so let me give you an example of a cognitive bias and its related heuristic. This is known as the anchoring heuristic, or the anchoring effect.

Kahneman and Tversky did a famous experiment in the early 1970s where they asked a group of subjects to estimate the percentage of countries in Africa that are members of the United Nations. Of course most aren't going to know this, for most of us this is just going to be a guess.

But for one group of subjects, they asked the question "Is this percentage more or less than 10 percent?" For another group of subjects, they asked the question "Is it more or less than 65 percent?"

The average of the answers of the two groups differed significantly. In the first group, the average answer was 25 percent. In the second group, the average answer was 45 percent. The second group estimated higher than the first group.

Why? Well, this is what seems to be going on. If subjects are exposed to a higher number, their estimates were "anchored" to that number. Give them a high number, they estimate higher; give them a lower number, they estimate lower.

So, the idea behind this anchoring heuristic is that when people are asked to estimate a probability or an uncertain number, rather than try to perform a complex calculation in their heads, they start with an implicitly suggested reference point—the anchor—and make adjustments from that reference point to reach their estimate. This is a shortcut; it's a rule of thumb.

Now, you might think in this case, it's not just the number; it's the way the question is phrased that biases the estimates. The subjects are assuming that the researchers know the answer and that the reference number is therefore related in some way to the actual answer. But researchers have redone this experiment many times in different ways.

In one version, for example, the subjects are asked the same question, to estimate the percentage of African nations in the United Nations, but before they answer, the researcher *spins a roulette wheel in front of the group*, wait for it to land on a number so they can all see the number, and then ask them if the percentage of African nations is larger or smaller than the number on the wheel.

The results are the same. If the number is high people estimate high, if the number is low people estimate low. And in this case the subjects couldn't possibly assume that the number on the roulette wheel had any relation to the actual percentage of African nations in the United Nations. But their estimates were anchored to this number anyway.

Results like these have proven to be really important for understanding how human beings process information and make judgments on the basis of information. The anchoring effect shows up in strategic negotiation behavior, consumer shopping behavior, in the behavior of stock and real estate markets—it shows up *everywhere; it*'s a very widespread and robust effect.

Note, also, that this behavior is, by the standards of our normative theories of correct reasoning, *systematically irrational.*

Linda Henman, Missouri-based business consultant, provides an example of when the anchoring effect can have a negative outcome: If a team leader asks his subordinates whether marketing efforts in a particular region should be increased by, say 20 percent, his employees will use that number as a cue. Perhaps the figure should be even higher, Henman notes, or the company needs to eliminate marketing efforts in that region altogether. By using the anchor of 20 percent, the boss has already planted a seed in his subordinates' minds, which will be difficult to erase.[3]

Why This Is Important

So this is an example of a cognitive bias. Now, this would be interesting but not deeply significant if the anchoring effect was the only cognitive bias that we've discovered. But if you go to the Wikipedia entry under "list of cognitive biases," you'll find a page that lists just *over a hundred* of these biases, and the list is not exhaustive. I encourage everyone to check it out.

So what's the upshot of all this for us as critical thinkers?

At the very least, we all need to acquire a certain level of cognitive bias "literacy." We don't need to become experts, but *we should all be able to recognize the most important and most discussed cognitive biases.* We should all know what "confirmation bias" is, what "base rate bias" is, what the "gambler's fallacy" is, and so on. *These are just as important as understanding the standard logical fallacies.*

Why? Because, as critical thinkers, we need to be aware of the processes that influence our judgments, especially if those processes systematically bias us in ways that make us prone to error and bad decisions ....

Chapter Takeaways

- A *cognitive bias* is a systematic error in judgment. A typical example of cognitive bias is *confirmation bias*, where we seek out or filter information so that it conforms to our own world view.
- Most of this book—the logical fallacies for example—focuses on prescriptive or normative rules of thinking; "Don't use logical fallacies!" But to become a good critical thinker, we need to know something about and be sensitive to how human beings reason. Studying cognitive biases is a good first step on this journey.
- Historically, marketers and economists viewed consumers as being logical decision-makers who sought to maximize value in their marketing transactions. The primary factors these social scientists studied were products, their features and benefits, and price.
- Since the 1970s, research has slowly accumulated in the fields of behavioral economics, neurology, and psychology, which strongly suggests that the consumer decision process is not only more complex than we thought it was, but is also affected by other factors such as the context in which consumers make decisions and the heuristics they use to simplify the decision process.
- We all need to acquire a basic level of cognitive bias literacy to truly become good critical thinkers. This and the following chapters give you a good introduction to this field. Additional suggested readings are given in the last chapter of this book.

CHAPTER 11

Science

A Tool for Reducing the Systematic Errors Caused By Cognitive Biases

(Consider the following) two points:

1. Human beings are prone to biases that lead to error.
2. Scientific methodology aims to neutralize the effects of these biases, and thereby reduce error.

Let's look at these two points in order.

First, human beings are prone to biases that lead to error. What sorts of biases? There are lots, but I'm thinking of two kinds of biases in particular.

In the context of this discussion, replace "marketing research" for "science." Marketing research uses the scientific method and the scientific way of thinking to generate knowledge about markets, thereby reducing systematic errors caused by cognitive biases.

We Are Pattern-Recognition Machines

The first (claim) is related to the fact that we're pattern-recognition machines. Human beings see patterns everywhere. We're bombarded by sensory data and our natural disposition is to seek out patterns in the data and a meaning to those patterns.

An obvious example of this is our tendency to see faces in anything that remotely resembles the configuration of features on a human face. An electrical outlet looks like a face, the front grill of a car looks like a face, the knots of a tree look like a face.

Now, it's not surprising that we see faces everywhere. Face recognition is important for social primates like us; it's very important that we learn to read the facial cues of other people to know whether they're friendly or a threat, whether they're content or displeased, and so on. So we've evolved this very specialized and sensitive mechanism for facial recognition, and as a result we're basically hard-wired for it.

But this means that we're prone to a certain kind of error as well, where *we see faces in inanimate things that don't really have faces.*

This is just one kind of pattern recognition mechanism working in our brains; there are lots of different kinds working all the time, looking for patterns that might be meaningful, and imposing meaning on those patterns if they trigger the right cues. Michael Shermer calls this feature of our mental functioning "patternicity."[1]

Now, in general, our ability to identify patterns is an extraordinarily valuable tool. It's essential for survival, for extracting meaningful, relevant information from our physical environment and from our social environment.

But there's a price we pay for this amazing ability—sometimes we attribute meaning to patterns that they don't have, and sometimes we see patterns in what is actually patternless noise. And it can be hard to not see these patterns when we expect to see them; our expectation, or the subconscious workings of our brain, can sometimes impose a meaningful pattern on data, or on sensory experience, even when there's nothing there.

Psychologists have a bunch of names for this phenomenon. For visual images, like seeing faces in clouds, or the Virgin Mary on a slice of burnt toast, it's called *pareidolia.* The general phenomenon is called *apophenia*, which is defined as the experience of seeing meaningful patterns or connections in random or meaningless data.

Here's a fun example.

Have you ever heard of *backmasking*? This is when you play an audio recording backward; usually these are songs, and you hear meaningful speech when it's played backward.

When you do this deliberately to an audio recording it's called "backmasking" or "backward masking." It was controversial in the 1980s when a number of Christian groups in the United States claimed that heavy metal rock bands were intentionally putting satanic messages into their songs, which people could hear if they played the songs backward.

What's interesting about backmasking is that people will often hear meaningful words or phrases in songs that are played backward, even when they were never intentionally put there. And the effect is amplified when you're given some cues about what to look for in the audio.

The very best place on the Internet to experience this effect is Jeff Milner's Backmasking site, at jeffmilner.com/backmasking.

On the video and audio versions of this lecture, I play a sample from Jeff's site to illustrate the effect, but I can't do that in a document. You can check Jeff's site for yourself, but what I did is play a sample from the Britney Spear's song "Hit Me Baby One More Time," first forward and then backward. The backward version sounds like incoherent noise to most ears. But when you prime the listener's expectations by showing them this set of lyrics: "Sleep with me, I'm not too young."

... (Then) play the backward sample again, (and) it is impossible *not* to hear those words. It's a striking effect (again, I urge you to go check it out).

Now trust me, Britney Spears didn't intentionally backmask those lyrics. This is meaningless noise being interpreted as meaningful information, and we're all prone to it, ... no amount of mental effort can make you not hear those lyrics ....

What does "backmasking" have to do with marketing, you might ask? Just show five different marketers the same Rorschach test (or an unfamiliar set of data), and ask them what they see! The problem is that, when we are given either incomplete (or massive amounts) of information, we strive to see patterns in that data—our brains try to make sense of things by imposing order, even if we are not consciously trying to do so. Since we each come to this interpretative task with different marketing experiences, successes, and failures that shape the lenses through which we interpret information, we see things differently. What to do about this? Seek second opinions. Debate issues. Examine the strength and cogency of differing arguments; conduct research. Additionally, ask yourself, "What kind of information might disprove my hypothesis?" And then try to find it.

One of the authors was privy to an experience that a large national retailer had in hiring two different consulting firms to build marketing mix models based on previous sales and advertising history. Using the same data set, the two respected consulting firms came up with two different marketing mix models! Admittedly, they did not completely contradict each other; but they were different enough to affect how the client might design its advertising strategy.

We Suck At Weighing Evidence

The second kind of error that we're prone to has to do with how human beings are naturally disposed to weigh evidence, and more specifically how we weigh evidence as it bears on the truth or falsity of a hypothesis.

The general error is this: If we think the hypothesis is true, or would like it to be true, then we tend to remember or focus only on the evidence that would count in favor of the hypothesis and ignore or dismiss evidence that would count against it.

The result is that as we build up a set of data that is lopsided in favor of the hypothesis that is biased toward confirmation. That's why this phenomenon is called confirmation bias, and there's a huge psychological literature on this.

Actually, "confirmation bias" can refer to a cluster of related phenomena. You can have:

1. **Biased search for information**: This is where people test hypotheses in a one-sided way, by only searching for evidence that is consistent with the hypothesis that they happen to hold. They ask, "What would you expect to see if this hypothesis was true?" and look for evidence to support this prediction, rather than ask, "What would you expect to see if this hypothesis was false?" and (then) look for evidence that would falsify the hypothesis.

2. **Biased interpretation of evidence**: This is where you give two groups the SAME information, the SAME evidence, but they interpret the evidence differently, depending on their prior beliefs. So if you strongly believe some hypothesis, then you'll be inclined to

think, for example, that studies that support that hypothesis are well-conducted and convincing; but for studies that don't support your hypothesis, you'll be inclined to think that they're not well-conducted, and not convincing. One way to think of this is that *people set higher standards of evidence for hypotheses that go against their current expectations, and they have lower standards of evidence for those that support their expectations.*

3. **Biased memory**: Even if someone has gone ahead and tried to collect evidence in a neutral, unbiased way, they may still remember it selectively, so *you end up recalling more of the confirming evidence than the disconfirming evidence*, and it skews the evidence in favor of your expectations.

I want to emphasize that these biasing effects I'm describing are well documented in the cognitive science literature; it's a part of the cognitive biases literature that goes back several decades now and it's an ongoing area of research.

Science Is What We Do to Keep Us from Lying to Ourselves

Okay, so what's the upshot of this for our understanding of science? The upshot is that, left to our own devices, human beings are prone to error in the weighing of evidence. What's the error? The error is thinking that we're making a judgment based on a complete body of evidence, when the body of evidence we're considering has actually been filtered and skewed by confirmation bias. And that's going to lead to error in judgments about how well supported a hypothesis actually is ....

Example: When Is A Correlated with B?

Let me give you a simple example to illustrate. Let's say you walk into a health care clinic and see a flyer for a psychotherapist's practice. The flyer says that *Dr. Jones has a 90 percent success rate in treating mental health problems.* You read a little more closely, and it says that of all the patients he sees who come to his clinic complaining of psychological or mental health problems, 90 percent of them report an improvement in their condition within two weeks of beginning treatment with Dr. Jones.

Now, for the sake of argument, let's assume this figure is accurate. If 100 people walk through his door suffering from some mental health problem, then if you survey them two weeks after beginning treatments with Dr. Jones, roughly 90 of them will say that their condition has improved.

Here's the first question: Does this evidence support the conclusion that Dr. Jones's treatment is *causally responsible* for the improvement in their condition?

I know from experience that if I ask my science students this question, about one-third will say that it does support this causal hypothesis, and about two-thirds will say "no," it doesn't, because they've been told many times in their psychology classes that correlation does not imply causation. Maybe there's some other factor involved that's responsible for the correlation; maybe it's the placebo effect, whatever. I think a survey of the general public would give a much stronger result, with a lot more people thinking that this evidence supports the claim that Dr. Jones' treatments are causally responsible for the improvement in condition.

Now, what if I ask this question? Let's grant that the correlation doesn't necessarily imply causation. But does the evidence given even support the weaker claim of a correlation? Does the fact that 90 percent of patients report (an) improvement of (their) condition support the claim that there's at least a correlation between Dr. Jones' treatments and the improvement in condition? And by correlation I just mean that if you go to Dr. Jones' clinic with a mental health problem, you're statistically more likely to report improvement in your condition than if you didn't seek out treatment.

If I ask this question to my science students, *almost all of them will say that the evidence supports some kind of correlation.* When I ask them how strong a correlation, more than half will say that it's 90 percent or close to 90 percent—that you're 90 percent more likely to report an improvement in your condition if you go see Dr. Jones.

Now, for those of you playing along at home, what do you think the answer is? Would you be surprised to hear that this evidence doesn't even support a claim of correlation? In fact, it gives us no reason to think there's any kind of correlation whatsoever, much less a 90 percent correlation!

Why is this? *It's because we're only looking at confirming evidence, we have no information about potentially disconfirming evidence.* To establish a correlation between Dr. Jones' treatments and improvement in condition, we would need to compare *two numbers*: the probability that a person will improve if they seek out treatment with Dr. Jones, and *the probability that they will improve anyway, on their own, without seeking treatment from Dr. Jones.*

If it turned out, for example, that 90 percent of people will report improvement in their mental health problems within two weeks *anyway*, without seeking treatment, then your odds of improving are the same whether you see Dr. Jones or not, and the correlation is *zero*, there's no positive correlation at all.

Or maybe there's an 80 percent rate of improvement without treatment, so if the rate of improvement is 90 percent, then at best this would support a weak positive correlation of 10 percent, which is still very different from a 90 percent correlation.

So, this evidence in Dr. Jones' flyer, even if it's all 100 percent accurate, not only does it not support the hypothesis that his treatments are the cause of the improvement in his patients' condition, *it doesn't even support a correlation of any kind between his treatments and improvement in his patients' condition.* There just isn't enough information to justify these claims. But almost none of my science students, when they're given this hypothetical case, will see that this is the case; most will say that the evidence supports a very strong correlation. This is because they're looking at an incomplete body of evidence and drawing a hasty inference, *but they don't realize until it's pointed out to them that the evidence is incomplete ....*

Let's face it. If an idea is ours, we seek out data to support its success or "correctness." If our idea is a flop, we seek out information to show that there were factors outside the organization's control that caused the failure. We are not being malevolent; it's just human nature. And to be good critical thinkers we need to own up to this fact. Statisticians and marketing researchers are really good at this because, with a sufficiently large database of information, almost any kind of "finding" can be discovered. This is not accidental. There is actually a term for it in the philosophy of science—it's called the under-determination of theories. This claim states that, for any given data set, there are an infinite number of possible explanations. Clearly, some explanations will be ridiculous. But many are often plausible.

Chapter Takeaways

- Cognitive biases are part of our human nature.
- We are pattern-recognition machines. We see patterns every-where. Again, this is part of our human nature.
- The problem for marketers is that, given a sufficiently large amount of information, the patterns we see are largely influenced by our backgrounds and experiences.
- Cognitive bias generally manifests itself in three activities: (1) searching for information that confirms our preconceptions; (2) filtering out information that supports our claims; and, (3) recalling facts and information that support our preconceived notions more readily than those that do not.
- Marketing research is a good tool to keep us from lying to ourselves.

CHAPTER 12

What Makes Science Special

I'd like to wrap up this lecture with a final comment on the bigger question that motivated this topic in the first place. The question was whether there's a way of defending the superiority of science as a source of knowledge about the world, without resorting to a mythic view of how science works.

I think the answer is "yes," but it's a qualified "yes." I think it's clear that if we didn't follow these scientific protocols, our knowledge of the world would be less reliable than it is, and it's clear why this is so when you think of these protocols as methods for neutralizing the effects of cognitive biases.

As you read the rest of this section, whenever you see the word "science," remember that marketing research is a social science. And good marketing research uses the same general methods as any science (e.g., experiments), approaches (relying on past research to inform future research); and techniques (e.g., mathematics and statistics) to discover insights about markets.

But saying this doesn't mean that scientists always follow these protocols. Science is a complex social practice, and there are lots of things that can interfere with or prevent these protocols from being properly implemented. The highest quality studies are often the most expensive studies to conduct, so funding can be a limiting factor. The highest quality studies might also take many years, maybe even decades to conduct, so time constraints can be another factor.

And, in some fields, proper controlled studies might just be impossible to conduct. In genetics, for example, there are experimental ways of measuring the heritability of a trait, which is the percentage of the variation in the trait that can be accounted for by genetic variation in the population. You can do these controlled experiments to directly measure heritability on fruit flies, but you can't do them on human populations because they would be unethical to conduct. So for humans we're forced to rely on more indirect methods of estimating heritability that are more limited and more vulnerable to biases.

So I admit that in some ways, this discussion of scientific methods still has an air of mythology about it, in the sense that it sets up an ideal that may never be perfectly realized in practice. But on the other hand, we still retain a notion of what makes science special, namely, that it's an institutionalized social practice that is committed to these ideals, that it strives to reduce the distorting effects of biases when it can. And in this respect it's distinctive; there's no other social institution that functions quite the same way ....

The Takeaway Message

So, the takeaway message of this ... is really fairly limited. It doesn't imply much for the big philosophical questions about the nature of science. But it does suggest a certain kind of attitude toward science, and the authority of science.

It suggests first of all, that people should be very cautious about relying on their intuitions in judging a scientific (or a marketing) issue. Our intuitions are just not reliable. One kid developing autism after a vaccination does not imply that the vaccine was the cause of the autism. But we all know that—the sample size is too small. What about 6,000 kids? Our intuition tells us that if 6,000 kids develop autism after being vaccinated, that's at least evidence for a strong correlation, right. *wrong*. It's evidence, but it's lop-sided, it's an incomplete body of data. Think of the Dr. Jones example.

When you actually look at a more complete body of data, including background rates of autism, the evidence is clear: there is no statistically significant correlation between vaccination and the development of autism. The number of reported cases of autism has certainly shot up over the past 30 years, but part of this is attributable to changes in diagnostic practices; how much of an increase there's been in the actual prevalence of the condition is still unclear, but there's no evidence that it's linked to vaccinations. Multiple studies from different scientific bodies agree on this conclusion.

Now, I know that a lot of people in the anti-vaccine movement resist this conclusion, and there are a lot of conflicted parents who see this as a tug-of-war between equal sides, an anti-vaccine side and a pro-vaccine side. But the takeaway message of this chapter is that the sides are not equal, and we shouldn't view them as equal. Human beings, left to their own devices, will see correlations where there aren't any, and attribute meaning to correlations that are actually meaningless. The more invested you are in the outcome, the more likely it is that you'll be led into error.

Only a proper scientific study can resolve the issue, and when multiple studies converge on the same conclusion, then the rational thing to do, provisionally, is to accept the scientific consensus ...

Chapter Takeaways

- Marketing research can be a defense against cognitive biases. When done well, marketing research borrows from science. *The scientific way of thinking* and *the scientific method* help marketers avoid cognitive biases and make good decisions.
- In the context of marketing, *the scientific way of thinking* is a method for understanding and explaining marketing phenomena that incorporates objectivity, systematic investigation, clarity of thought (especially regarding the definitions and concepts it seeks to understand), and knowledge gained from all relevant fields of study.
- In the context of marketing, *the scientific method* is a process by which theories are developed and tested for their ability to explain and enhance our understanding of marketing phenomena.
- Marketing research (and science) is what we do to keep us from lying to ourselves.

CHAPTER 13

Confirmation Bias and the Evolution of Reason

Last lecture I talked a lot about *confirmation bias*, this tendency we have to filter and interpret evidence in ways that reinforce our beliefs and expectations. And I argued that one way to think about science and scientific methodology is as a set of procedures that function to neutralize the distorting effects of confirmation bias (among other cognitive biases) by forcing us to seek out and weigh even the evidence that might count against our beliefs and expectations.

There are two sides to cognitive bias research. There's the science that *describes the effects of these biases* on our judgment and behavior, and there's the science that tries to *explain why* we behave in this way, that tries to uncover the psychological or neurological or social *mechanisms that generate* the behavior.

Everyone agrees that confirmation bias is a very real phenomenon; the descriptive part is well established. But not everyone agrees on the *explanation* for why we're so prone to this bias, what *mechanisms* are at work to generate it. And when there's disagreement at this level, there can be disagreement about how to best counteract the effects of confirmation bias. So *as critical thinkers we should be interested in these debates, for this reason, and because they're relevant on a deeper level to how we should think of ourselves as rational beings* ....

An Evolutionary Explanation of Confirmation Bias

So from this perspective, we can ask the broad question, *why* did human reason evolve? And by "reason" here I mean a very specific ability, namely, *the ability to generate and evaluate arguments, to follow a chain of inferences, and to construct and evaluate chains of inferences that lead to specific conclusions.* Human rationality can be defined much more broadly than this, but we're focusing on this specific component of rationality for the time being.

Now, if we assume that this ability to construct and evaluate arguments is an evolutionary adaptation of some kind, the question then becomes, what is this ability an adaptation *for?*

The Simple and Obvious Story

Well, here's one simple and obvious way to think about it. Our ability to construct and evaluate arguments evolved because it has *survival value*, and it has survival value because it helps us to arrive at *truer beliefs* about the world, and to *make better decisions* that further our goals. This ability to reason is a general purpose tool for constructing more accurate representations of the world and making more useful and effective decisions. We assume that, in general, ancestral humans that are better able to reason in this way will have a survival advantage over those that don't. So we expect that a higher percentage of individuals with this trait will survive and reproduce, and over time the trait will come to dominate the population, and that's why the trait evolved and persists in human populations.

Confirmation Bias: A Problem for the Simple and Obvious Story

Now, if we accept this simple story, then we have an immediate problem. The problem is that when we look at the psychological literature, we see that *human beings are often very bad at following and evaluating arguments, and they're often very bad at making decisions.* This is the take-home message of a good deal of the cognitive bias research that's been conducted over the past 40 years!

To take the obvious example, human beings are systematically prone to confirmation bias. Confirmation bias leads us to disproportionately accept arguments that support our beliefs and reject arguments that challenge our beliefs, and this leads to errors in judgment; we think our beliefs are more justified than they really are.

Now, from this simple evolutionary stance, the existence of confirmation bias is a bit of a puzzle. If reason evolved to improve the quality of our individual beliefs and decisions, then what explains the persistence of confirmation bias, and other cognitive biases that undermine the quality of our individual beliefs and decisions?

The Argumentative Theory of Reason

The new approach to these questions that is getting some recent attention tries to resolve this puzzle about confirmation bias. It's known as the argumentative theory of reason, and it claims that the central adaptive function of human reasoning is to generate and evaluate arguments within a social setting, to generate arguments that will convince others of your point of view, and to develop critical faculties for evaluating the arguments of others.

Now this might not seem like a radical hypothesis, but I want you to note the contrast between this view and the previous one we just described. The previous view was that the central adaptive function of human reason was to generate more accurate beliefs and make better decisions for individuals. In other words, the function is to improve the fit between individual beliefs and the world, resulting in a survival advantage to the individual.

The argumentative theory of reason rejects this view, or at least it wants to seriously modify this view. It says that human reason evolved to serve social functions within human social groups.

What are these functions?

Well, imagine two ancestral humans who are trying to work together, to collaborate to find food, defend against aggressors, raise children, and so on. This all works fine when both parties agree on what they want and how to achieve it. But if a disagreement arises, then their ability to work together is compromised. They need to be able to resolve their disagreement to get back on track.

Now let's imagine that this pair of ancestral humans lacks the ability to articulate the reasons for their respective views, or the ability to evaluate the reasons of the other. They're stuck, they can't resolve their disagreement, and because of this, their collaboration will probably fail and their partnership will dissolve.

Now imagine another pair of ancestral humans in the same situation who have the ability to articulate and evaluate their reasons to one another. They have the potential to resolve their disagreement through mutual persuasion. This pair is more likely to survive as a pair, and to reap the benefits of collaboration.

And for this reason, this pair will likely out-compete groups or individuals who lack the ability to argue with one another. And according to this theory, that's the primary reason why the ability to reason evolved in human populations—to serve the needs of collaboration within social settings, not to improve the quality of individual beliefs or to track the truth about the world.

How the Argumentative Theory Explains Confirmation Bias

The argumentative theory of reason is the product of two French researchers, the well-known anthropologist and cognitive psychologist Dan Sperber and his former student Hugo Mercier.[1]

One of the reasons they offer in support of their theory is that it helps to explain the existence of confirmation bias.

How does it do this? Let's walk through this, it's kind of interesting.

In a social setting where there are lots of different individuals with different beliefs and values, everyone is required to play two roles at different times, the role of the *convincer*—the one who is giving the argument that is intending to persuade—and the role of the *convincee*—the one who is the recipient of the argument and the intended object of persuasion.

Now, if your goal as a convincer is to use reason to persuade others, then a bias toward confirming arguments and confirming evidence is going to serve you well. As a convincer your goal *isn't* the impartial weighing of evidence to get at the truth, *it's to assemble reasons and evidence that will do the job of persuading others to accept your conclusion.*

Adroit use of confirmation bias may partially explain successful politicians and executives who climb the corporate ladder quickly.

Things are different when you're the convincee, the one who is the object of persuasion. In this context you can imagine two extreme cases for how you should handle these attempts to persuade you. On the one hand, you could decide to accept everything that other people tell you. But that's not going to serve your needs very well—*you'll be pulled in different directions, you won't have stable beliefs, and you won't be effective at asserting your own point of view.*

On the other hand, you could decide to reject everything that other people tell you that doesn't conform to your beliefs. This is the ultra-dogmatic position—you stick to your guns come what may. This has some obvious advantages. You'll have a stable belief system, you'll attract collaborators who think they way you do, and so on.

But it's still not ideal, because *the ultra-dogmatic stance runs the risk of rejecting arguments with true conclusions that would actually improve their condition if they were to accept them.*

A better compromise position is one where there's a default dogmatism, where your initial reaction is to resist arguments that challenge your beliefs, but this default dogmatism is tempered by a willingness and ability to evaluate arguments on their merits, and thereby make yourself open to rational persuasion.

From an evolutionary standpoint, this compromise position, which you might call "moderate dogmatism," seems to offer the maximum benefits for individuals and groups.

Now when you combine the optimal strategy of the convincer, which is biased toward arguments and evidence that support your beliefs, and the optimal strategy of the convincee, which is biased against arguments and evidence that challenge your beliefs, *you end up with an overall strategy that looks an awful lot like the confirmation bias that psychologists have been documenting for decades.*

And this is what Sperber and Mercier are saying. When we think of reason as serving the goals of social persuasion, confirmation bias shouldn't be viewed as a deviation from the proper function of human reason. Rather, it's actually a constitutive part of this proper function, this is what it evolved FOR. To use a computer software analogy, confirmation bias isn't a "bug," it's a "feature."

Consequences of This View

Now, I don't know if this view is right. But I do find it provocative and worth thinking about. I mentioned earlier that different views on confirmation bias can result in different views of how best to neutralize or counteract it. Sperber and Mercier argue that their view has some obvious consequences along these lines.

For one, their view implies that *the worst case scenario is individuals reasoning alone in isolation.* Under these conditions we're most prone to the distorting effects of confirmation bias.

A much better situation is when individuals *reason in groups* about a particular issue. This way everyone can play both the role of the convincer and the convincee, and we can take advantage of our natural ability to evaluate the quality of other people's arguments, and others can evaluate the quality of our arguments. We should expect that reasoning in groups like this will result in higher quality judgments than reasoning in isolation, and lots of studies on collective reasoning do bear this out.

> *Next time you're in a group setting debating a marketing issue, have one or a few colleagues play the Devil's Advocate and try to show that the prevailing inductive argument is weak and not cogent. (Remember, nearly all marketing arguments are inductive, not deductive, arguments.) "Weak" in this context means that, assuming true premises, the conclusion does not logically follow. "Cogent" means the argument's premises are true, or at least plausible to your audience. If time allows, give them time to research the subject matter and come back to the group with their strongest counter-arguments. This approach can be helpful in "war gaming" your competitors' responses to your marketing mix.*

But of course not all groups are equal. If a group is very homogeneous, with lots of shared beliefs and values and background assumptions, then the benefits of group reasoning are more limited because there are collective confirmation biases that won't be challenged.

So, if we're looking to *maximize the quality of our judgments and our decisions*, the better situation is when the groups are not so homogenous, when there's *a genuine diversity of opinion represented within the group*, and you can expect that at least some people will start off disagreeing with you. Under these conditions, the benefits of group reasoning and group argumentation are greatest—the result will be judgments that are least likely to be distorted by confirmation bias ....

Chapter Takeaways

- What causes confirmation bias? It may be some baggage that we're carrying from our evolutionary past.
- Developing short-cut mechanisms for decision-making and pattern-recognition abilities likely helped our ancestors avoid lions and other dangerous predators. But what worked in the jungle may not work in the boardroom. Relying on fixed decision rules and pattern-recognition abilities may lead us down the wrong path.
- Another explanation for confirmation bias weaknesses likes in the Argumentative Theory of Reason. Learning how to develop and evaluate arguments in a social setting gave small human groups the skills they needed to cooperate and survive.
- One of the best ways to counter our natural inclination toward confirmation bias is to discuss topics in *heterogeneous* groups. If everyone has similar backgrounds and experiences, not much will be challenged. Try to assemble people with different backgrounds and experiences.
- Why should you care about this? There are at least two reasons. First, because to the extent that we, as critical thinkers, are aware of the factors that bring about cognitive biases, we will be less likely to use them to develop weak or invalid arguments. Second, having a basic understanding of how evolutionary forces may have contributed to this situation gives us a better understanding of our nature as human beings.

CHAPTER 14

Epistemic Humility

If we know that we're prone to confirmation bias, but that this bias can be neutralized by following certain scientific protocols, or by reasoning together in diverse groups, then this can lead to strategies for effectively managing and reducing the effects of this bias.

Also, if we know that we're prone to confirmation bias, and we know that we're also prone to overconfidence, then it helps us to identify certain attitudes, or virtues, that should be cultivated to help avoid the effects of these biases.

One of these attitudes is what I like to call epistemic humility. "Epistemic" is a philosopher's term that means "pertaining to knowledge," so in this respect I'm talking about humility regarding the status of our knowledge and our capacity to reason well.

Now, this isn't the same as skepticism about *knowledge*—to be epistemically humble isn't necessarily to *doubt* our knowledge, or to deny the possibility of knowledge. It's rather to adopt an epistemic stance that is appropriate to, and that acknowledges, our situation as fallible, limited beings that are prone to overconfidence and error.

The degree to which we're prone to error will vary from context to context. The key idea here is that the quality of our judgments is highest when our epistemic stance—the attitude we take toward our own status and capacities as knowers—properly matches the epistemic environment in which we find ourselves. For example, if we're reasoning all by ourselves, this is a different epistemic environment than if we're reasoning with a diverse group of people. Given what we know about reasoning, it's appropriate to adopt a greater degree of epistemic humility when we're reasoning by ourselves than when we're reasoning with a diverse group.

And sometimes the appropriate stance is simply to not trust our own judgments at all. That's an extreme form of humility, but in the right circumstances it can be the most rational stance to take.

A classic example of this kind of rational humility can be found in the Greek story of Odysseus and the Sirens. The Sirens were these mythic female creatures who sang these beautiful songs that lured sailors into the water … (crashing) their boats onto the shores of their island.

Odysseus was very curious to know what the Siren song sounded like, but he understood that he may not be able to resist their song. So he did something very clever; he had all his sailors plug their ears with beeswax and tie him to the mast. He ordered his men to leave him tied tightly to the mast, no matter how much he might beg to untie him.

When he heard the Sirens' beautiful song he was overcome by it and he desperately wanted to jump into the sea to join them, and as he predicted he ordered the sailors to untie him. But they refused based on his earlier orders. So, *as a result of his strong sense of rational humility regarding his own capacity to resist persuasion, Odysseus was able to experience the Sirens' song and come out unscathed, where other men with less humility were lured to their deaths.*

For critical thinkers the moral of this parable is clear. Although it may seem counterintuitive, by accepting and even embracing our limitations and failings as cognitive agents, rather than denying them or struggling against them, it's possible to improve the quality of our judgments and make more rational decisions than we would otherwise. But to pull this off we need to cultivate the right kind of epistemic virtues that are informed by the right kind of background knowledge, and through knowledge and experience, learn to develop the appropriate judgment about the right level of epistemic humility to adopt in any particular circumstance.

From a marketer's point of view, there is a practical problem associated with being epistemically humble—time! Events and circumstances often conspire to take away available time to ponder and research our arguments. There never seems to be enough of it to make good decisions; although marketers are forced to find time to fix the bad ones.

An example of this was when Fresh Market, a specialty grocery chain, rushed the decision to open a store in Des Moines, Iowa, in October 2015, only to close it seven months later.[1] Although we're speculating somewhat, Fresh Market did not seem to have grasped the level of competition in this market for fresh fruits and vegetables from Hy-Vee, a regional grocery store chain, or the other already established specialty grocery stores, Trader Joe's and Whole Foods. Statements about Fresh Market's future competition would have formed part of the premises of their argument to open a Des Moines store.

At the heart of Fresh Market's decision to open their Iowa location lies the remnants of a collection of poor premises—known only to its senior executives—supporting their argument's weak and likely uncogent conclusion: "Therefore, we should open a store in Des Moines, Iowa."

Chapter Takeaways

- *Epistemic humility* is being "mindful of our innate reasoning shortcomings and striving to make fewer reasoning errors by using good, truth-conducive reasoning tools."[2]
- Epistemic humility does not mean that we are skeptical of our ability to generate *knowledge*—justified, true-beliefs. It just means that we are humble about our ability to do so.
- A major obstacle that confronts our ability to act with epistemic humility is *time*. The pressures of the day-to-day business world and the various demands on our schedules conspire to force us not to take the time required, or invest the resources needed, to construct good arguments. Therefore, we too often find ourselves falling back on unreliable decision-making heuristics and undependable gut reactions to solve marketing problems.
- It seems that there is never enough time to make sound and cogent arguments; yet we are forced to make time to clean up our mistakes. Find the logic in that!

SECTION III

Conclusions

CHAPTER 15

Summary

The Logical Fallacies and Think Better sections of this book cover nearly 100 "do's" and "don'ts" on how to be a better critical thinker. After finishing the draft of the book, even the authors wondered, *"How am I going to remember all this stuff?"* We offer three tips: (1) use the critical thinking checklist provided below, (2) take slightly more time to construct your marketing arguments on a day-to-day basis, and (3) continue your learning by checking out the suggested critical thinking resources in the next chapter.

The Critical Thinking Checklist

Photocopy and cutout for easy reference!

Critical Thinking Checklist for Marketing Arguments

1. Are your premises understandable (e.g., clear sentences, defined terms)?
2. Do you have good evidence for each premise?
3. Are your argument's premises true or plausible to your audience?
4. Are your premises logically linked to your conclusion?
5. Do your premises have implied premises that should be made explicit to make your argument more persuasive? Repeat #1–4 for each implied premise that you've made explicit.
6. Is your conclusion understandable and believable?

Are Your Premises Understandable?

A number of logical fallacies address this issue directly or indirectly—Argument by Gibberish, Ambiguity Fallacy, and Lying with Statistics—as does the Think Better piece, "What is a Concept?" Avoiding jargon, using the same definition for a word or phrase consistently, and avoiding vague or ambiguous language, will take you a long way in constructing understandable premises for your marketing arguments.

Do You Have Good Evidence for Your Premises?

What constitutes "good" evidence? First let's define *evidence*: That which is used to support an argument. "Good" evidence, therefore, is support that helps persuade your audience. Good evidence is:

- *Relevant*: The support is pertinent to the argument's conclusion. Marketing research can provide relevant support to an argument for increasing a product's price; "gut feel" does not. Also, avoid hearsay; it may be interesting, but hearsay is not good evidence.
- *Verifiable*: Can the evidence be substantiated by your audience? Not that anyone will want to take the time to do this, but knowing that one can substantiate a claim adds credence to your evidence. Also, it's a way of double-checking yourself.
- *Sufficient*: Assess sufficiency from two perspectives. First, have you covered all relevant topics? For example, if you are arguing to expand the sales force, some relevant topics to cover might focus on appropriate measures of sales force workload, sales potential forecasts, and sales force effectiveness.[1] Second, has each topic been covered at a sufficient depth? For example, if you are making an argument to improve product quality, have you defined all the dimensions of product quality (e.g., durability, reliability, product life) and made clear which aspects of product quality you are recommending to improve?
- *Accurate*: Accuracy is the extent to which a statement faithfully reflects some aspect of the world. If you make the

argument, say, to expand digital media expenditures, and as part of your argument, you claim that all of your competitors use digital media, is that claim accurate—is it truly 100 percent, or is it more like 90 percent or 80 percent?

As discussed in the Think Better piece, "Marketing Arguments," good critical thinking does not demand that premises be true with a capital "T," but they do need to be as accurate as is possible and plausible to your audience.

Accuracy is related to trustworthiness. Your audience will not believe in the accuracy of your source if they don't trust it, no matter that your source may have used advanced or "scientific" methods to generate the evidence you're using (e.g., see The Ludic fallacy and Lying with Statistics).

Are Your Premises True or Plausible to Your Audience?

To discover any credibility gaps in advance, try out your argument on a friend or colleague before making a formal presentation.

For example, senior sales managers in a large chemical manufacturer were initially skeptical of certain marketing research finding. The credibility of the research was significantly enhanced when the investigator explained how respondents were properly screened in the survey process. Management needed to be made comfortable that the research interviewed the proper decision makers in the firms interviewed.

Are Your Premises Logically Linked to Your Conclusion?

Recall that the Non Sequitur fallacy (literal meaning, "does not follow") addresses this weakness in arguments, which, after reading this book, you are not likely to use. Rather, the goal here is to make your arguments as *strong* as possible. Recollect that the definition of a strong inductive argument is: If the premises are true, the conclusion is highly likely. So ask yourself, "How can I make my argument *stronger*?"

There are various ways to do this. For example, are your premises sufficient—both in the number of relevant issues covered and also the depth to which each is developed? For example, in making an argument to expand a product line, some of your premises might examine issues such as trial, repeat volume, and market penetration of brands in the current product portfolio. You might be able to strengthen your argument further by addressing additional measures of product portfolio performance such as year-on-year growth, cannibalization rates, and various brand equity metrics.

Do Your Premises Have Implied Premises That Should Be Identified to Make Your Argument More Persuasive?

Watch out for this one! All premises have, in varying degrees, unstated premises that can go on forever. Stop when you have grounds to believe that the premise you're developing has been sufficiently flushed out to be plausible for your audience. Consider Figure 15.1.

In the first example (middle column), claiming that "annual sales will continue to grow by 7 percent" implies that "what occurred in the past will continue in the future." The implied premise incorporates David Hume's "problem of induction," discussed in the Think Better piece, "David Hume."

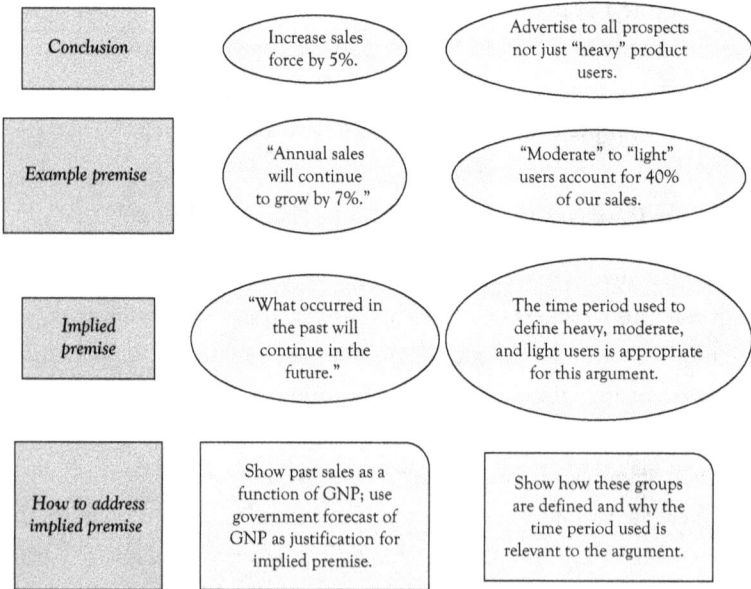

Figure 15.1 Stated and implied premises

It's best in this case to give some justification for this implied premise. One way is to note that the company's growth rate is affected by the overall economy and that there is a strong statistical relationship between the company's growth rate and gross national product (GNP). Then refer to a reliable economic forecasting source's projections of GNP (for our U.S. readers, this is the Federal Reserve Bank).

In the second example, the premise "moderate to light users account for 40 percent of our sales" is evidence used to support the conclusion that the firm needs to "advertise to all prospects, not just 'heavy' users." The implied premise here is that the time period used to create the heavy, moderate, and light user groups is appropriate for this argument. One can affect the percentage of moderate and light users in a given market simply by shortening the time frame to create the categories. For example, the percentage of light users in a given category increases as the time frame increases. The appropriate time frame is a function of how often, on average, consumers purchase a product. Therefore, demonstrate to your audience that the time frame to create these categories is appropriate (e.g., one year for most consumer packaged goods; maybe five years for certain industrial equipment goods).

You probably have recognized that the chain of implied premises can go on nearly forever. Where do you stop? In the first example, we suggest that a second premise that's used to support the Example Premise might be:

> We can expect annual sales growth to increase by 7% because, over the past 10 years, average GNP growth has been 3%, and our company's growth, accounting for adding new stores, has always been 2.3 times GNP growth, and the Federal Reserve forecasts GNP growth over the next five years at 4%.

You might want to provide further evidence supporting the claim that company growth will continue to be 2.3 times GNP growth.

When do you stop supporting your premises? Clearly, one has to use judgment. Remember, a good argument will persuade your audience. Flush out as many implied premises you feel are necessary to make your argument strong and cogent to your audience.

Is Your Conclusion Understandable?

This is likely to become an issue if the conclusion is vague or ambiguous. For example, if your conclusion is, "We need to improve the quality of our products?" what does "quality" mean, what does "improve" mean?

Make sure your conclusion is reasonable, given the context of your industry. If your conclusion calls for an outcome that your industry has never experienced—for example, "Therefore we need to increase our sales force 300 percent over the next three months"—you'd better have very compelling premises and logic to support it.

Take More Time to Make Decisions

This may be the most difficult recommendation to incorporate into your day-to-day work schedule. Most of us are doing the job of at least one-and-a-half, if not two other people. And when the clock strikes 5:00 p.m. (or 1700 hours for our international and military readers), most of us would just rather be at home with our families. Nevertheless, we encourage you to try, for three reasons: (1) mistakes are time-consuming and expensive, (2) you'll get more efficient at critical thinking over time, and (3) as you perfect your critical thinking skills over time, you can become a mentor to others.

Mistakes Waste Time and They Can Be Expensive

Often it takes more time to fix a mistake than it does to do a job right the first time. *"If you don't have time to do it right, when will you have time to do it over?"*[2] JCPenney provides the classic example:

> By the turn of the New Year in 2012, JCPenney was struggling to stay afloat. The department store fought to stand out amongst competitors, so CEO Ron Johnson decided to take a new approach: to eliminate "sales" and "fake prices." Instead, they would make everyday prices reflect what used to be sales prices, and they wouldn't price items ending in 9 (for example, $7.99)

but would use whole figures. It appears that customers preferred to feel *like* they were getting a bargain, because JCPenney's revenue dropped 25% that year, and almost 20,000 employees had to be laid off.[3]

The bottom line: Over the long run, improving and using your critical thinking skills will save time. "A stitch in time saves nine."

The "stitch in time" is simply the prompt sewing up of a small hole or tear in a piece of material, so saving the need for more stitching at a later date when the hole has become larger. Clearly the first users of this expression were referring to saving nine stitches.[4]

You Will Get More Efficient Over Time

One of the reasons we included 60 logical fallacies in our book is that by examining critical thinking from many different perspectives, you begin to develop a better feel, or "sixth sense" for when you're tempted to use poor reasoning in an argument—or if you are the target of a logical fallacy. Make a game of it. Next time you listen to a politician (especially a politician), advertising on the radio or TV, or a colleague at work, keep your critical thinking antenna attuned to what you're hearing. Just by being sensitive, you'll find that, over time, identifying logical fallacies will become second nature. You'll be able to assess others' arguments, and make your own arguments quicker.

Become a Mentor to Others

Many readers are either in management or will enter management's ranks in the future. As Virgin Atlantic's Richard Branson said:

When talking about the importance of mentoring, the American author and businessman Zig Ziglar couldn't have said it any better—"A lot of people have gone further than they thought they could because someone else thought they could." Ask any successful businessman and, if they are honest about it, they will almost certainly admit to having benefited from the advice of a mentor at some point along the way.[5]

We can think of no better way to mentor others than to help them improve their critical thinking skills. Help those in your team to learn how to think, as well as what to think!

CHAPTER 16

Additional Readings

One useful way to fine-tune your critical thinking antenna is to learn more about critical thinking and the field of cognitive biases. In this light, we strongly recommend that you visit Kevin deLaplante's website, whose work we've referenced earlier, and whose website offers a treasure trove of critical thinking resources: http://kevindelaplante.com/. Also, sign up to the Critical Thinking for Marketers group on LinkedIn.

Additionally, the following list of books comes from a combination of suggested readings from Kevin's website and the resources of this book's authors. They range across a variety of fields—critical thinking, psychology and cognitive biases, psychology and persuasion, and marketing and marketing theory. Many of these books can be purchased on Amazon. com for a fraction of their original cost.

Creative Thinking and Critical Thinking

- Kaufman, Scott Barry and Carolyn Gregoire, (2015). *Wired to Create: Unraveling the Mysteries of the Creative Mind.* New York: Perigee.
- Michalko, Michael, (2006). *Tinkertoys: A Handbook of Creative-Thinking.* New York: Ten Speed Press.
- Weston, Anthony, (2007). *Creativity for Critical Thinkers.* London: Oxford University Press.

Critical Thinking Textbooks

- Baillargeon, Charb, (2007). *A Short Course in Intellectual Self-Defense.* New York: Seven Stories Press.
- Epstein, Richard and Michael Rooney, (2012). *Critical Thinking.* New York: Advanced Reasoning Forum.

- Groarke, Leo and Christopher W. Tindale, (2008). *Good Reasoning Matters!* (5th Ed.). Ontario, Canada: Oxford University Press.
- Kelly, David, (2014). *The Art of Reasoning: An Introduction to Logic and Critical Thinking.* New York: W.W. Norton & Company.
- LeBlanc, Jill, (1998). *Thinking Clearly: A Guide to Critical Thinking.* New York: W.W. Norton & Company.
- Salmon, Merrilee H., (2007). *Introduction to Logic and Critical Thinking* (5th Ed.). Belmont, CA: Thompson Wadsworth.

Marketing and Marketing Theory

- Grapentine, Terry, (2012). *Applying Scientific Reasoning to the Field of Marketing: Make Better Decisions.* New York: Business Expert Press.
- Sharp, Byron, (2010). *How Brands Grow: What Marketers Don't Know.* Victoria, Australia: Oxford University Press.
- Sharp, Byron, (2016). *How Brands Grow: What Marketers Don't Know, Part 2.* Victoria, Australia: Oxford University Press.
- Sharp, Byron, (2013). *Marketing: Theory, Evidence, Practice.* Victoria, Australia: Oxford University Press.
- Zaltman, Gerald, Christian R. A. Pinson and Reinhard Angelmar, (1973). *Metatheory and Consumer Research.* New York: Holt, Rinehart and Winston, Inc.

Psychology and Cognitive Biases

- Ariely, Dan, (2008). *Predictably Irrational, Revised and Expanded.* New York: HarperCollins.
- Kahneman, Daniel, (2009). *Thinking, Fast and Slow.* New York: Farrar, Straus and Giroux.
- Nisbett, Richard E., (2015). *Mindware: Tools for Smart Thinking.* New York: Farrar, Straus and Giroux.

- Tavris, Carol and Elliot Aronson, (2015). *Mistakes Were Made (but not by Me): Why We Justify Foolish Beliefs, Bad Decisions, and Hurtful Acts.* New York: Houghton Mifflin Harcourt.

Psychology and Persuasion

- Brown, Derren, (2009). *Tricks of the Mind.* Transworld Digital.
- Cialdini, Robert B. (2009). *Influence: Science and Practice* (5th Ed.). New York: Pearson.
- Kolenda, Nick, (2013). *Methods of Persuasion: How to Use Psychology to Influence Human Behavior.* Kolenda Entertainment, LLC.
- Smith, Nicholas J.J., (2012). *Logic: The Laws of Truth.* Oxfordshire, UK: Princeton University Press.
- Thaler, Richard H., and Cass R. Sunstein, (2008). *Nudge: Improving Decisions About Health, Wealth, and Happiness.* London: Penguin Books.

Notes

Chapter 1

1. Stanford Encyclopedia of Philosophy (2005).
2. Google (n.d.).
3. *Wikipedia* (n.d.). Retrieved from http://en.wikipedia.org/wiki/Heuristic

Chapter 2

1. deLaplante (2016).
2. Farris et al. (2006, 26).
3. Belch and Blech (2001, 152).
4. Belch and Blech (2001, 152).
5. Farris et al. (2006, 26).
6. Farris et al. (2006, 26).
7. Sharp (2010, 7).
8. Sharp (2010, 7).
9. LeBlanc (1998, 303).
10. Grapentine (2012, 10).
11. Grapentine (2012, 10).

Chapter 3

1. Baggozzi (1980, 1).
2. Malhotra (2012, 220).
3. Baggozzi (1980, 17–18).

Chapter 4

1. Giese and Cote (2000).
2. Grapentine and Teas (2008).

Chapter 6

1. Sharp (2013, 112).
2. Sharp (2013, 112).
3. Sharp (2010).

Chapter 7

1. North, Hargreaves, and McKendrick (1999).

Chapter 8

1. SixSigma (n.d.).
2. *Wikipedia* (n.d.). Retrieved from http://en.wikipedia.org/wiki/5_Whys

Chapter 9

1. *Wikipedia* (2012). https://en.wikipedia.org/wiki/Cognitive_bias
2. deLaplante (2016).

Chapter 10

1. Kahneman (2011).
2. Jaccard and Jacoby (2010, 48).
3. Sarfin (n.d.).

Chapter 11

1. Shermer (2008).

Chapter 13

1. Mercier and Sperber (2011).

Chapter 14

1. Johnson (2016).
2. Grapentine (2012, 209).

Chapter 15

1. Farris et al. (2006, 158–59).
2. Dachis (2016).
3. Nazar (2013).
4. The Phrase Finder (n.d.).
5. Branson (2016).

References

Baggozzi, R.P. 1980. *Causal Models in Marketing*. New York: John Wiley & Sons.

Baldoni, J. January 20, 2010. *How Leaders Should Think Critically*. Cambridge, MA: Harvard Business Review. Retrieved from http://blogs.hbr.org/2010/01/how-leaders-should-think-criti/

Belch, G.E., and M.A. Belch. 2001. *Advertising and Promotion*. New York: McGraw-Hill Irwin.

Branson, R. 2016. *The Importance of Having a Mentor in Business*. Virgin. Retrieved from www.virgin.com/richard-branson/the-importance-of-having-a-mentor-in-business

Dachis, A. 2011. "If You Don't Have Time To Do it Right, When Will You Have Time To Do it?" Retrieved from http://lifehacker.com/5818760/if-you-dont-have-time-to-do-it-right-when-will-you-have-time-to-do-it-over

deLaplante, K. 2016. "Critical Thinking Academy: Learn to Think Like a Philosopher." Retrieved from www.udemy.com/critical-thinker-academy/#%2F

Farris, P.W., N.T. Bendle, P.E. Pfeifer, and D.J. Reibstein. 2006. *Marketing Metrics: 50+ Metrics Every Executive Should Master*. Upper Saddle River, NJ: Pearson Education, Inc.

Giese, J.L., and J.A. Cote. 2000. "Defining Customer Satisfaction." *Academy of Marketing Science Review* 2000, no. 1, pp. 1–24. Retrieved from www.researchgate.net/profile/Joan_Giese/publication/235357014_Defining_consumer_satisfaction/links/5419a5790cf203f155ae0afb.pdf

Google. n.d. "Behavioral Economics." Retrieved from www.google.com/webhp?sourceid=chrome-instant&ion=1&espv=2&ie=UTF-8#q=behavioral+economics

Grapentine, T. 2009. "What Really Affects Behavior?" *Marketing Research Magazine: A Magazine of Management and Applications,* Winter, 12–18.

Grapentine, T. 2012. *Applying Scientific Reasoning to the Field of Marketing: Make Better Decisions*. New York: Business Expert Press.

Grapentine, T., and R.K. Teas. 2008. "What's really important?" *Marketing Research Magazine: A Magazine of Management and Applications,* Summer, 18–27.

Jaccard, J., and J. Jacoby. 2010. *Theory Construction and Model-Building Skills*, 48. New York: The Guilford Press.

Johnson, P. May 4, 2016. "The Fresh Market to close Iowa stores." *The Des Moines Register*, p. 12A.

Kahneman, D. 2011. *Thinking Fast, and Slow*. New York: Farrar, Straus and Giroux.

LeBlanc, J. 1998. *Thinking Clearly: A Guide to Critical Reasoning*. New York: W.W. Norton & Company.

Malhotra, N.K. 2012. *Basic Marketing Research: An Applied Orientation*. Englewood Cliffs, NJ: Prentice Hall.

Mercier, H., and D. Sperber. 2011. "Why do Humans Reason? Arguments for an Argumentative Theory." *Behavioral and Brain Sciences* 34, no. 2, pp. 57–74.

Nazar, J. 2013. "The Biggest Business Blunders in History." Business Insider. Retrieved from www.businessinsider.com/the-biggest-business-blunders-in-history-2013-11

North, A.C., D.J. Hargreaves, and J. McKendrick. April 1999. "The Influence of In-Store Music on Wine Selections." *Journal of Applied Psychology* 84, no. 2, pp. 271–76.

Sarfin, R.L. n.d. "Anchoring Effects to Influence Decision Making in Business." Houston Chronical. Retrieved at http://smallbusiness.chron.com/anchoring-effects-influence-decision-making-business-23427.html

Sharp, B. 2010. *How Brands Grow: What Marketers Don't Know*. Victoria, Australia: Oxford University Press.

Sharp, B. 2013. *Marketing: Theory, Evidence, Practice*. Victoria, Australia: Oxford.

Shermer, M. 2008. "Patternicity: Finding Meaningful Patterns in Meaningless Noise: Why the Brain Believes Something is Real When it is Not." Scientific American. Retrieved from www.scientificamerican.com/article/patternicity-finding-meaningful-patterns/

SixSigma. n.d. "Determine the Root Cause: The 5 Whys." Retrieved from www.isixsigma.com/tools-templates/cause-effect/determine-root-cause-5-whys/

Stanford Encyclopedia of Philosophy. 2005. "Epistemology." Retrieved from http://plato.stanford.edu/entries/epistemology/

The Phrase Finder. n.d. "The Meaning and Origin of the Expression: A Stitch in Time Saves Nine. Retrieved from www.phrases.org.uk/meanings/a-stitch-in-time.html

Wikepedia. n.d. "Heuristic." Retrieved from https://en.wikipedia.org/wiki/Heuristic

Index

OTHER TITLES IN OUR MARKETING STRATEGY COLLECTION

Naresh Malhotra, Georgia Tech, Editor

- *Sales Promotion Decision Making: Concepts, Principles, and Practice* by Steve Ogden-Barnes and Stella Minahan
- *Smart Marketing: How to Dramatically Grow Your Revenue* by Ahmed Al Akber
- *Market Sensing Today* by Melvin Prince and Constantinos-Vasilios Priporas
- *Launching New Products: Best Marketing and Sales Practices* by John Westman and Paul Sowyrda
- *Marketing Plan Templates for Enhancing Profits* by Elizabeth Rush Kruger
- *Relationship Marketing Re-Imagined: Marketing's Inevitable Shift from Exchanges to Value Cocreating Relationships* by Naresh K. Malhotra, Can Uslay, and Ahmet Bayraktar
- *Service Excellence: Creating Customer Experiences that Build Relationships* by Ruth N. Bolton
- *Critical Thinking for Marketers: Learn How to Think, Not What to Think, Volume I* by David Dwight, Terry Grapentine, and David Soorholtz

Announcing the Business Expert Press Digital Library

Concise e-books business students need for classroom and research

This book can also be purchased in an e-book collection by your library as

- a one-time purchase,
- that is owned forever,
- allows for simultaneous readers,
- has no restrictions on printing, and
- can be downloaded as PDFs from within the library community.

Our digital library collections are a great solution to beat the rising cost of textbooks. E-books can be loaded into their course management systems or onto students' e-book readers. The **Business Expert Press** digital libraries are very affordable, with no obligation to buy in future years. For more information, please visit **www.businessexpertpress.com/librarians**. To set up a trial in the United States, please email **sales@businessexpertpress.com**.

www.ingramcontent.com/pod-product-compliance
Lightning Source LLC
Chambersburg PA
CBHW071111210326
41519CB00020B/6266